1

NE_Build & Grow

Unit Components

Student Book

Build Your Vocabulary
This helps students to learn key words in context through engaging sentences and illustrations.

Think Together
Students have the chance to think about the unit's main theme and express their opinions. This helps to draw students' attention before the main reading.

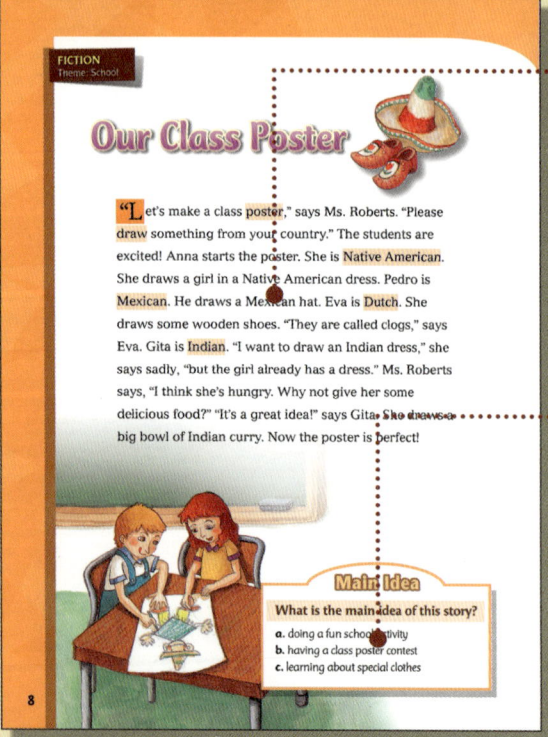

Main Text
Fiction and nonfiction stories are paired in one theme. Compelling, theme-based topics are presented to stimulate students' intellectual curiosity.

Main Idea
A quick question after the main passage tests students' understanding of the reading.

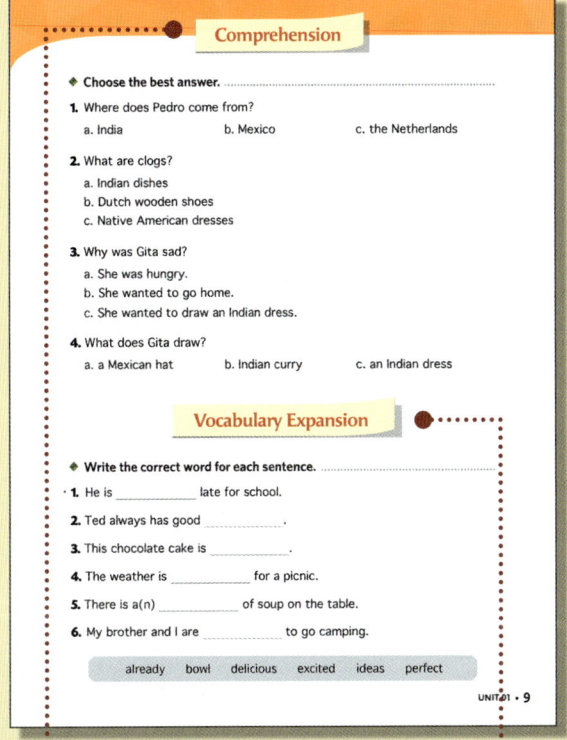

Comprehension

◆ Choose the best answer.

1. Where does Pedro come from?
a. India　　　　b. Mexico　　　　c. the Netherlands

2. What are clogs?
a. Indian dishes
b. Dutch wooden shoes
c. Native American dresses

3. Why was Gita sad?
a. She was hungry.
b. She wanted to go home.
c. She wanted to draw an Indian dress.

4. What does Gita draw?
a. a Mexican hat　　　b. Indian curry　　　c. an Indian dress

Vocabulary Expansion

◆ Write the correct word for each sentence.

1. He is _____ late for school.

2. Ted always has good _____.

3. This chocolate cake is _____.

4. The weather is _____ for a picnic.

5. There is a(n) _____ of soup on the table.

6. My brother and I are _____ to go camping.

| already | bowl | delicious | excited | ideas | perfect |

UNIT 01 · 9

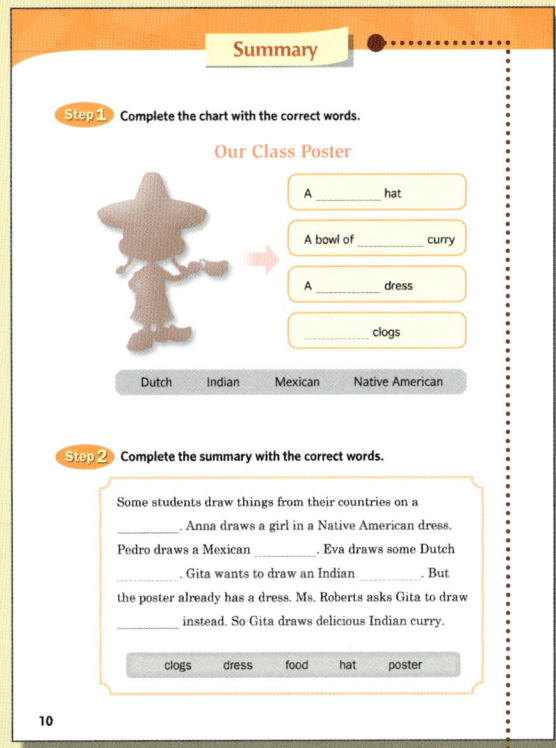

Summary

Step 1 Complete the chart with the correct words.

Our Class Poster

A _____ hat

A bowl of _____ curry

A _____ dress

_____ clogs

| Dutch | Indian | Mexican | Native American |

Step 2 Complete the summary with the correct words.

Some students draw things from their countries on a _____. Anna draws a girl in a Native American dress. Pedro draws a Mexican _____. Eva draws some Dutch _____. Gita wants to draw an Indian _____. But the poster already has a dress. Ms. Roberts asks Gita to draw _____ instead. So Gita draws delicious Indian curry.

| clogs | dress | food | hat | poster |

10

Reading Comprehension

Additional questions about the main passage further check students understanding of the reading and strengthen students' reading accuracy.

Vocabulary Expansion

Additional key words are presented in different contexts to further expand students' vocabulary.

Summary

Different types of summarizing activities will help students improve their ability to create a strong, accurate summary of the main passage.

Workbook

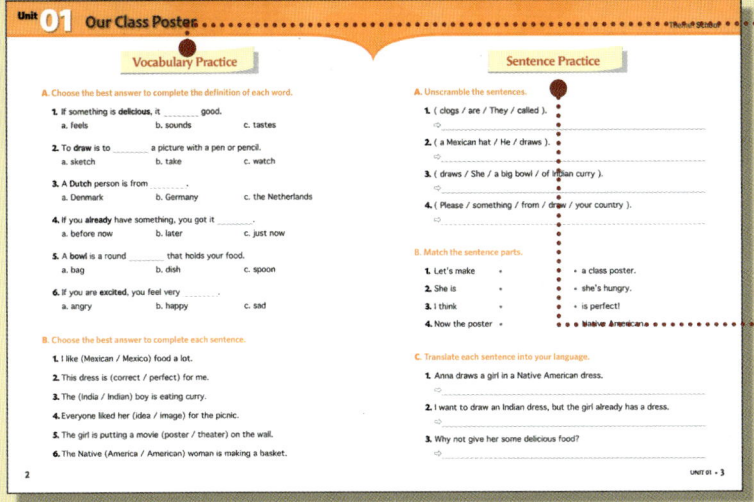

Vocabulary Practice

Definitions and meaningful sentences using key words from the unit give the students more practice.

Sentence Practice

Exercises focusing on sentence structure enhance students' reading and writing skills.

Contents

Our Class Poster

Build Your Vocabulary

◆ **Match the sentences to the correct letters in the picture.**

1. There is a **poster** for the party on the wall. _____

2. The boy **draws** a picture. _____

3. The **Mexican** boy is wearing a hat. _____

4. The **Indian** girl gives food to a boy. _____

5. The **Dutch** girl is wearing wooden shoes. _____

6. The **Native American** girl is wearing a brown dress. _____

Think Together Look at the picture and check Yes, No, or Don't know.

	Yes	No	Don't know
1. The students wear special clothes for a party.	☐	☐	☐
2. The students come from different countries.	☐	☐	☐

Our Class Poster

"Let's make a class poster," says Ms. Roberts. "Please draw something from your country." The students are excited! Anna starts the poster. She is Native American. She draws a girl in a Native American dress. Pedro is Mexican. He draws a Mexican hat. Eva is Dutch. She draws some wooden shoes. "They are called clogs," says Eva. Gita is Indian. "I want to draw an Indian dress," she says sadly, "but the girl already has a dress." Ms. Roberts says, "I think she's hungry. Why not give her some delicious food?" "It's a great idea!" says Gita. She draws a big bowl of Indian curry. Now the poster is perfect!

Main Idea

What is the main idea of this story?

a. doing a fun school activity
b. having a class poster contest
c. learning about special clothes

Comprehension

◆ **Choose the best answer.** ....

1. Where does Pedro come from?

    a. India   b. Mexico   c. the Netherlands

2. What are clogs?

    a. Indian dishes
    b. Dutch wooden shoes
    c. Native American dresses

3. Why was Gita sad?

    a. She was hungry.
    b. She wanted to go home.
    c. She wanted to draw an Indian dress.

4. What does Gita draw?

    a. a Mexican hat   b. Indian curry   c. an Indian dress

Vocabulary Expansion

◆ **Write the correct word for each sentence.** ....

1. He is _____ late for school.

2. Ted always has good _____.

3. This chocolate cake is _____.

4. The weather is _____ for a picnic.

5. There is a(n) _____ of soup on the table.

6. My brother and I are _____ to go camping.

| already | bowl | delicious | excited | ideas | perfect |

Step 1 Complete the chart with the correct words.

Our Class Poster

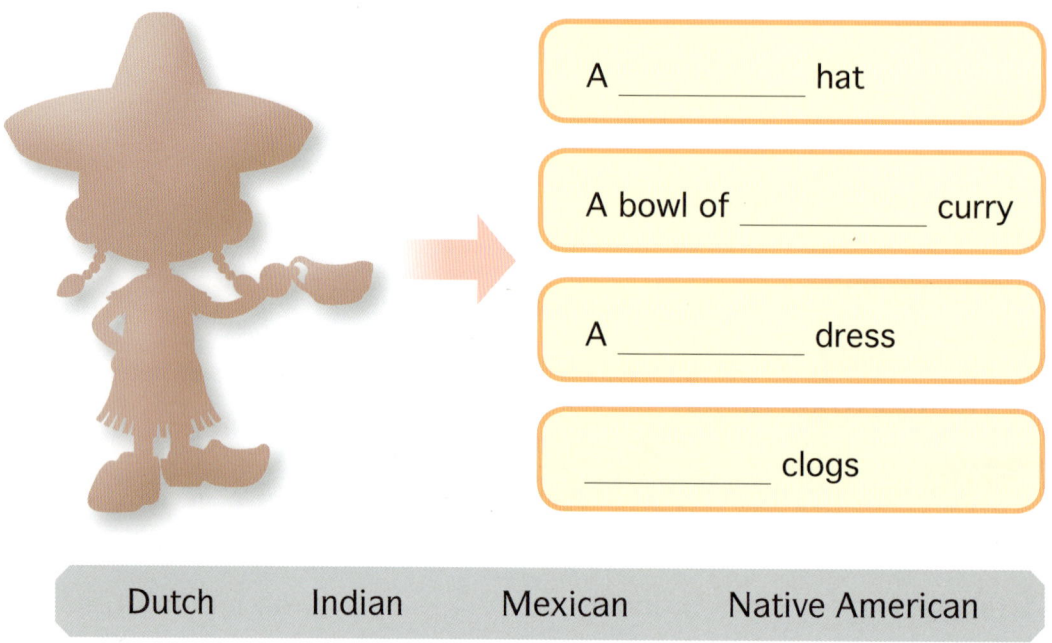

A _____ hat

A bowl of _____ curry

A _____ dress

_____ clogs

| Dutch | Indian | Mexican | Native American |

Step 2 Complete the summary with the correct words.

Some students draw things from their countries on a _____. Anna draws a girl in a Native American dress. Pedro draws a Mexican _____. Eva draws some Dutch _____. Gita wants to draw an Indian _____. But the poster already has a dress. Ms. Roberts asks Gita to draw _____ instead. So Gita draws delicious Indian curry.

| clogs | dress | food | hat | poster |

The 100th Day of School

Build Your Vocabulary

◆ **Match the sentences to the correct letters in the picture.**

1. The **stamps** are in the bag. _____

2. The teacher is wearing a **necklace**. _____

3. There is a box of **cereal** on the table. _____

4. They have a **special** day of activities on Friday. _____

5. The girls **bring** photos to school. _____

6. They have **regular** classes from Monday to Thursday. _____

Think Together Look at the picture and check Yes, No, or Don't know.

	Yes	No	Don't know
1. The students are having an art class.	☐	☐	☐
2. The students bring special things today.	☐	☐	☐

The 100th Day of School

The 100th day of school is a special day in elementary schools around the United States. American schools start in September. So the 100th day is usually in February. It is a day of fun and learning. Students do not have regular classes. Instead, they enjoy games and activities based on the number 100! For example, they may make necklaces from 100 pieces of cereal. Or they may draw pictures of themselves at age 100. They may bring 100 special things to school for show and tell. The 100 things may be photos, stamps, crayons, or anything! What do you want to bring on your 100th day of school?

Main Idea

What is the main idea of this text?

a. a special day at school
b. studying math at school
c. learning about the number 100

Comprehension

♦ **Choose the best answer.** ....

1. Who celebrates the 100th day of school?

    a. high school students

    b. middle school students

    c. elementary school students

2. When does the 100th day of school usually happen?

    a. in February   b. in May   c. in September

3. What do students do on the 100th day of school?

    a. take a test   b. enjoy activities   c. have regular classes

4. What is NOT true about the 100th day of school?

    a. Students bring 100 things to school.

    b. Students count from 1 to 100 together.

    c. Students draw pictures of themselves at age 100.

Vocabulary Expansion

♦ **Write the correct words for each sentence.** ....

1. I have five _____ today.

2. Cooking is always _____.

3. I want a(n) _____ of cake.

4. What did you do at my _____?

5. My sister and I are _____ students.

6. He is drawing a(n) _____ of his mom.

age   classes   elementary school   fun   picture   piece

Step 1 Complete the chart with the correct words.

The 100th Day of School

Where	in _____ schools
When	in _____
What	enjoy games and _____ based on the number 100
How	· make _____ · _____ pictures · bring special things for show and tell

activities   draw   elementary   February   necklaces

Step 2 Complete the summary with the correct words.

The 100th day of school is a _____ day in American elementary schools. It is usually in February. On that day, there are no _____ classes. Instead, there are fun activities _____ on the number 100. For example, students may _____ 100 things for show and tell. The 100 things may be photos, _____, crayons, or something else!

based   bring   fun   regular   stamps

14

Welcome to Nest House

Build Your Vocabulary

◆ **Match the sentences to the correct letters in the picture.**

1. The birds **find** a new house. _____

2. The girl and the man made a **birdhouse**. _____

3. The birdhouse is made of **wood**. _____

4. There are some eggs in the **nest**. _____

5. The bird eats a **seed** from the man's hand. _____

6. The girl **welcomes** the birds to her birdhouse. _____

Think Together Look at the picture and check Yes, No, or Don't know.

	Yes	No	Don't know
1. The birds don't like the birdhouse very much.	☐	☐	☐
2. Not many birds live in the city.	☐	☐	☐

Welcome to Nest House

Emily is making a birdhouse with her dad. They make the birdhouse out of wood. It has a little door and windows. And it has a place for food and water. Emily's dad says that birdhouses are important. He says, "There aren't many birds in cities these days. They can't find safe places for their nests. But this birdhouse is a safe place. Birds can live in it and have babies." Emily wants to welcome many birds. So she puts seeds and fruits in the birdhouse. She even gives it a name. She calls it Nest House. "Come on, birds," she says. "Come to Nest House!"

Main Idea

What is the main idea of this story?

a. making a home for birds
b. finding birds' nests in cities
c. having birds in your house

◆ **Choose the best answer.** ....

1. What is the birdhouse made of?

  a. grass   b. wood   c. plastic

2. What does the birdhouse NOT have?

  a. a door and windows
  b. a sign for the house name
  c. a place for food and water

3. Why aren't there many birds in cities now?

  a. because they can't find any food
  b. because they don't like noisy places
  c. because they can't find safe places for their nests

4. What does Emily put in the birdhouse?

  a. seeds and fruits   b. fruits and nuts   c. nuts and seeds

Vocabulary Expansion

◆ **Write the correct word for each sentence.** ....

1. Is it _____ to swim in this lake?

2. London is a big _____ in England.

3. I have a very _____ exam tomorrow.

4. This park is a good _____ for a picnic.

5. Please don't _____ your bag on the table.

6. My grandmother always _____ me her "little angel."

| calls | city | important | place | put | safe |

Step 1 Complete the chart with the correct words.

```
                                    is made of _____

                                    has a door and _____

      Emily's
      Birdhouse                     has a place for _____
                                    and water

                                    is a _____ place to live in
                                    and have _____
```

| babies | food | safe | windows | wood |

Step 2 Complete the summary with the correct words.

Emily and her dad are making a _____ out of wood. It has a door, windows, and a place for food and water. It is a safe _____ for birds to live in and have babies. Emily puts _____ and fruits in the birdhouse to _____ many birds. She also gives the birdhouse a _____ – Nest House.

| birdhouse | name | place | seeds | welcome |

18

Homes for Earth Lovers

Build Your Vocabulary

◆ **Match the sentences to the correct letters in the picture.**

1. The house looks like a **cave**. _____

2. The **walls** are made of mud. _____

3. There is a **bathroom** in the house. _____

4. There is a small garden on the **roof**. _____

5. You can grow **plants** in the garden. _____

6. The flower pots are on the **ground**. _____

Think Together **Look at the picture and check Yes, No, or Don't know.**

	Yes	No	Don't know
1. It is always dark in this house.	☐	☐	☐
2. It will be fun to live in this house.	☐	☐	☐

Homes for Earth Lovers

An earth house is a new kind of home. You can find it in Switzerland. It is under the ground, so it looks like a cave or a fairy house. Why do people build earth houses? It is because earth houses can save energy in many ways. First, an earth house is built in the earth and has mud walls. So it stays warm in winter and cool in summer. Second, the bathroom has roof windows. Plenty of natural light comes in through the windows. Also, an earth house has grass on the roof. You can grow many plants and pretty flowers there. Isn't it great?

Main Idea

What is the main idea of this text?

a. Earth houses save energy.
b. You can save energy at home.
c. People in Switzerland save energy.

Comprehension

◆ **Choose the best answer.** ....

1. Where can you find an earth house?

    a. in the mud   b. in a forest   c. under the ground

2. What are the walls of an earth house made of?

    a. mud   b. wood   c. stone

3. What is NOT true about an earth house?

    a. It is in Switzerland.

    b. It has roof windows.

    c. It stays cold in winter.

4. What is on the roof of an earth house?

    a. a door   b. grass   c. rocks

Vocabulary Expansion

◆ **Write the correct words for each sentence.** ....

1. Wind energy is _____ energy.

2. I think subways can _____ time.

3. He drinks _____ water every day.

4. What _____ of sports do you like?

5. After the rain, we played in the _____.

6. My parents _____ tomatoes on their farm.

| grow | kind | mud | natural | plenty of | save |

Summary

Step 1   Complete the chart with the correct words.

An Earth House

Design

1. _____ walls

2. _____ windows

3. grass on the roof

Good Things

1. _____ in winter and cool in summer

2. plenty of natural _____ comes in

3. grow many _____ and pretty flowers

light   mud   plants   roof   warm

Step 2   Complete the summary with the correct words.

There is a new kind of home in Switzerland. It is called an earth house. It is under the ground. It has mud _____, so it stays warm in winter and _____ in summer. And it has roof windows in the bathroom, so _____ light comes in through the windows. Also, there is _____ on the roof. You can grow plants and _____ there.

cool   flowers   grass   natural   walls

A Little Help from Your Friends

Build Your Vocabulary

◆ **Match the sentences to the correct letters in the picture.**

1. The boy is wearing a **shirt**. _____

2. The boy **drops** a book. _____

3. There are tubes of **paint** on the table. _____

4. The students **share** a sandwich. _____

5. The girl **chooses** a book from the shelf. _____

6. There are many books in the **library**. _____

Think Together **Look at the picture and check Yes, No, or Don't know.**

	Yes	No	Don't know
1. The books are too heavy for the boy.	☐	☐	☐
2. No one wants to help the boy.	☐	☐	☐

A Little Help from Your Friends

Yesterday, many bad things happened to Tim. At the school library, Tim chose six books. But it was too many and he dropped them. But his friend Anita came over. She carried some books for him. Tim smiled and thanked her. At lunch, Tim opened his bag. "Oh no!" he said. "I forgot my lunch!" But his friend Mike said, "That's okay. You can share my lunch with me." Later, in art class, Tim got paint all over his T-shirt. Luckily, his friend Alex gave him a soccer shirt to wear. Tim felt so happy. Thanks to his kind friends, his bad day became a good day!

Main Idea

What is the main idea of this story?

a. Friends cannot always help you.
b. With friends, bad days can get better.
c. Good things only happen to good kids.

Comprehension

◆ **Choose the best answer.** ....

1. Who helped Tim in the library?

    a. Anita   b. Mike   c. Alex

2. What did Tim forget to bring to school?

    a. his books   b. his lunch   c. his school bag

3. How did Alex help Tim during art class?

    a. He gave Tim a shirt.

    b. He helped Tim clean up.

    c. He shared paint with Tim.

4. How did Tim feel when Alex helped him?

    a. sorry   b. happy   c. lucky

Vocabulary Expansion

◆ **Write the correct word for each sentence.** ....

1. I always _____ his name.

2. Can I _____ your T-shirt?

3. I have some _____ news.

4. Mark is smart and very _____.

5. The man _____ the police officer.

6. Can you help me _____ these boxes?

bad   carry   forget   kind   thanked   wear

Summary

Step 1 Complete the chart with the correct words.

Tim's Bad but Good Day

Bad Things

1. Tim _____ the books.

2. Tim forgot his lunch.

3. Tim got _____ on his T-shirt.

Friends' Help

1. Anita _____ some books for Tim.

2. Mike _____ his lunch with Tim.

3. Alex gave Tim his soccer _____.

| carried | dropped | paint | shared | shirt |

Step 2 Complete the summary with the correct words.

Many _____ things happened to Tim yesterday. He dropped all his _____, but Anita carried some of them. He _____ his lunch, but Mike shared _____ with him. Then he got paint on his T-shirt. But his friend Alex gave him a shirt. Tim's kind friends all _____ him. And his bad day became a good day!

| bad | books | food | forgot | helped |

26

Build Your Vocabulary

◆ **Match the sentences to the correct letters in the picture.**

1. The girl is wearing a **colorful** T-shirt. _____

2. The girl is wearing three **bracelets**. _____

3. The bracelet has many **knots**. _____

4. The bracelet is a sign of **friendship**. _____

5. The boy's bracelet **broke**. _____

6. The girl's dress has a flower **pattern**. _____

Think Together **Look at the picture and check Yes, No, or Don't know.**

	Yes	No	Don't know
1. Many people give a bracelet to their friends.	☐	☐	☐
2. If your bracelet breaks, you will have bad luck.	☐	☐	☐

A Sign of True Friendship

A friendship bracelet is a special sign of friendship. Today, giving a friendship bracelet is popular among teenagers. A friendship bracelet is very colorful. And it has many knots in different patterns. Its knots mean that true friendship cannot break. It takes a long time to make a bracelet. So, a friendship bracelet shows that you love and care for a special friend. In fact, it is a Native American tradition. You make a bracelet and give it to your friend. Then the friend wears the bracelet until it breaks. Do you want to keep your best friend forever? Then how about making a friendship bracelet for your friend?

Main Idea

What is the main idea of this text?

a. the importance of true friendship
b. the meaning of a friendship bracelet
c. a popular birthday gift among teenagers

◆ **Choose the best answer.**

1. What does a friendship bracelet NOT have?

    a. a lot of knots   b. special stones   c. different colors

2. What do the knots in a friendship bracelet mean?

    a. True friends are very close.
    b. True friendship never breaks.
    c. True friends are always together.

3. What does a friendship bracelet show?

    a. love and care   b. luck and money   c. health and happiness

4. What is NOT true about a friendship bracelet?

    a. It is popular among adults.
    b. It takes a long time to make it.
    c. It is a Native American tradition.

Vocabulary Expansion

◆ **Write the correct word for each sentence.**

1. A jacket _____ you warm.

2. What does this word _____?

3. Smiling is a _____ of happiness.

4. Mike is _____ among his friends.

5. Jane doesn't _____ for noisy music.

6. Our family has a special _____ at Christmas.

| care | keeps | mean | popular | sign | tradition |

Summary

Summary

Step 1 Complete the chart with the correct words.

is _____ among teenagers

A Friendship Bracelet

is very _____ and has different _____

shows love and _____ for a friend

is a Native American _____

care   colorful   patterns   popular   tradition

Step 2 Complete the summary with the correct words.

Friendship bracelets are popular among _____. They are colorful bracelets with many knots. The knots make _____ patterns. Friendship bracelets _____ as a Native American tradition. You make a friendship bracelet and give it to a friend to _____ love and care. Then the friend _____ it until it breaks.

different   show   started   teenagers   wears

30

A Boy Cheerleader's Story

Build Your Vocabulary

◆ **Match the sentences to the correct letters in the picture.**

1. The boys are **cheerleaders**.　　　　_____

2. Three boys **practice** the same moves.　　_____

3. The boy **jumps** in the air.　　　　_____

4. The **strong** boy holds up another boy.　_____

5. The boy **twists** his body in the air.　_____

6. The fathers are **proud** of all the boys.　_____

Think Together Look at the picture and check Yes, No, or Don't know.

	Yes	No	Don't know
1. Cheerleading takes a lot of practice.	☐	☐	☐
2. There are not many boy cheerleaders.	☐	☐	☐

A Boy Cheerleader's Story

My name is Kyle and I am a boy cheerleader. That's right – I said a boy cheerleader! Maybe you think cheerleading is only for girls. Actually, cheerleading is a very active sport. Like other sports players, cheerleaders are fit and strong. We practice our skills a lot. We run, jump, and twist in the air. Cheerleading is a team sport, so we learn to move together in rhythm. At first, my dad didn't like it. He said, "Why can't you play football instead?" But then he watched me cheerleading at a football game. He said, "Wow!" Then I felt so proud. I love cheerleading so much!

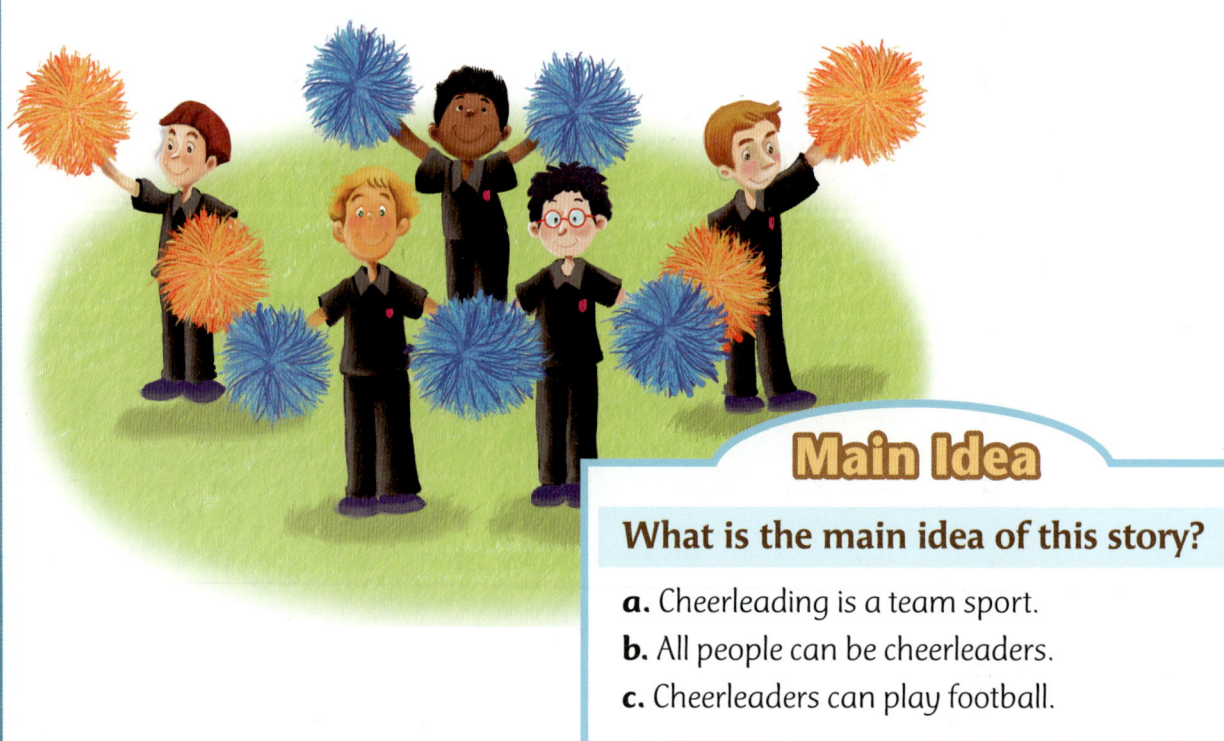

Main Idea

What is the main idea of this story?

a. Cheerleading is a team sport.
b. All people can be cheerleaders.
c. Cheerleaders can play football.

◆ **Choose the best answer.**

1. What are cheerleaders like?

    a. fit and strong   b. fast and smart   c. handsome and kind

2. What do cheerleaders do a lot?

    a. play sports together   b. practice their skills   c. watch football games

3. When did Kyle's dad change his mind about cheerleading?

    a. when he tried cheerleading

    b. when he read a book about cheerleading

    c. when he watched Kyle cheerleading at a football game

4. What is NOT true about cheerleading?

    a. It is a team sport.

    b. It is a very active sport.

    c. It is popular among boys.

Vocabulary Expansion

◆ **Write the correct word for each sentence.**

1. Swimming is a very _____ sport.

2. They _____ television after dinner.

3. Mark runs every day, so he is _____.

4. Today, computer _____ are important.

5. My little brother always _____ too slowly.

6. The students all dance in _____ at the party.

| active | fit | moves | rhythm | skills | watch |

Summary

Step 1 Complete the chart with the correct words.

Cheerleading

An Active Sport	A Team Sport
· cheerleaders are fit and _____ · cheerleaders _____ their _____ a lot	· cheerleaders learn to _____ together in _____

move   practice   rhythm   skills   strong

Step 2 Complete the summary with the correct words.

My name is Kyle and I'm a boy _____. Cheerleading is a very _____ sport. Cheerleaders are _____ and strong and we practice our skills a lot. Cheerleading is a(n) _____ sport, so we learn to move together. At first, my dad didn't like cheerleading. But he _____ his mind after he watched me cheerleading.

active   changed   cheerleader   fit   team

34

Sliding Stones on the Ice!

Build Your Vocabulary

◆ **Match the sentences to the correct letters in the picture.**

1. There are four **players** on a team. _____

2. The woman **slides** the stone on the ice. _____

3. The woman holds the **brush** in her right hand. _____

4. The woman **sweeps** the ice. _____

5. The **target** has a red ring in the center. _____

6. The World Women's Curling **Championship** is held here. _____

Think Together Look at the picture and check Yes, No, or Don't know.

	Yes	No	Don't know
1. The women are cleaning the ice.	☐	☐	☐
2. The stone moves to the target.	☐	☐	☐

Sliding Stones on the Ice!

W hich sport has ice, big stones, and long brushes? It is a winter sport called curling! Curling has two teams of four players. Each team has eight stones. One Player slides the stones to the target on the ice. The other players sweep the ice. This helps the stones move closer to the target. Players cannot touch the stones with their brushes. Curling is popular in Canada, the U.S., the U.K., Northern Europe, and Japan. The World Curling Championships are held each year. Curling players believe in fair play. So they always follow the rules. If you want to play a fun and unusual game, try curling!

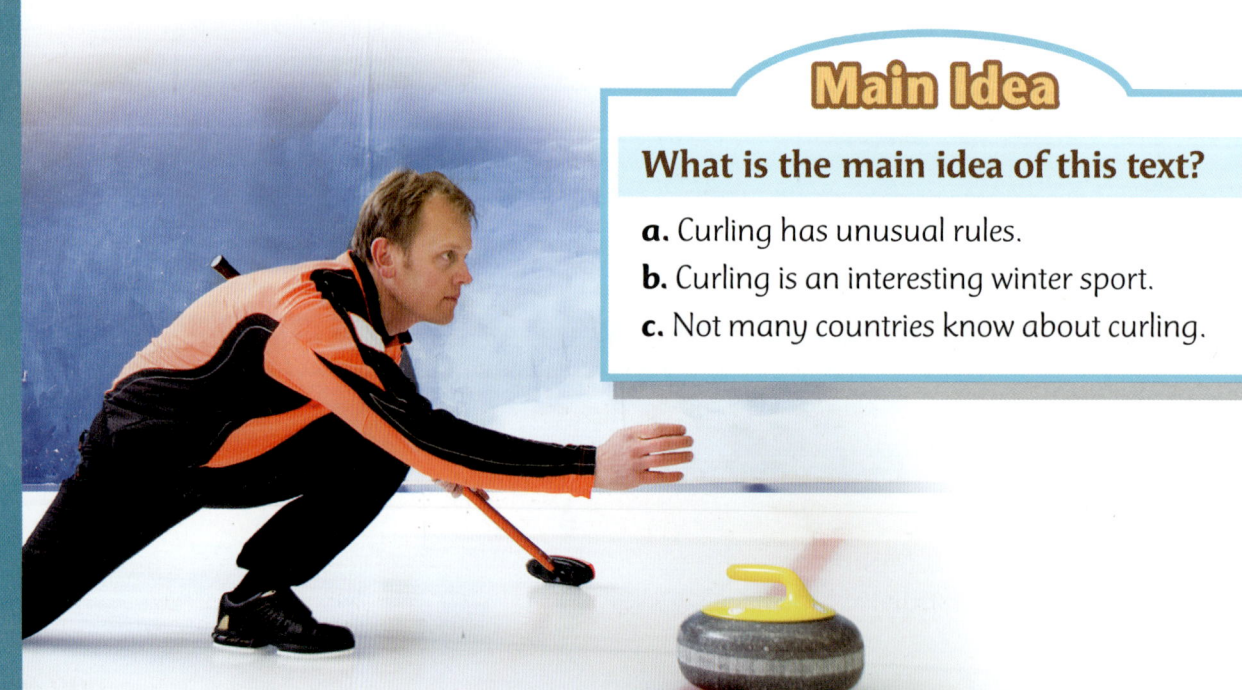

Main Idea

What is the main idea of this text?

a. Curling has unusual rules.
b. Curling is an interesting winter sport.
c. Not many countries know about curling.

Comprehension

◆ **Choose the best answer.** ....

1. How many players are there on one curling team?

    a. two   b. four   c. eight

2. What do players do with the long brushes?

    a. They sweep the ice.

    b. They push the stones.

    c. They clean up the floor.

3. How often are the World Curling Championships held?

    a. every month   b. every year   c. every four years

4. What is true about curling?

    a. It is popular in many Asian countries.

    b. Players slide the stones to the target.

    c. Players can touch the stones with their brushes.

Vocabulary Expansion

◆ **Write the correct word for each sentence.** ....

1. I _____ my friend's advice.

2. Many people _____ in UFOs.

3. Let's _____ bungee jumping!

4. It is very cold in _____ Europe.

5. The _____ of the game are simple.

6. The coach teaches _____ play to the players.

| believe | fair | followed | Northern | rules | try |

Step 1 Complete the chart with the correct words.

Curling

What You Need
- two teams of _____ players
- eight _____
- long brushes

How You Play
- _____ the stones
- _____ the ice to make the stones move toward the target

Other Facts
- the World Curling Championships happen _____ year
- players believe in _____ play

| each | fair | four | slide | stones | sweep |

Step 2 Complete the summary with the correct words.

In curling, there are two teams of four _____. Each team has eight stones. Players slide the stones on the ice, and sweep the _____ with their brushes. It makes the stones slide to the _____. Curling is _____ in some countries. The World Curling Championships are held each year. And curling players like to play fairly, so they always _____ the rules.

| follow | ice | players | popular | target |

Healthy Vegetable Soup

Healthy Soup
the ingredients:
4 potatoes
3 carrots
1 pumpkin
1 onion
Salt, spices

Build Your Vocabulary

◆ **Match the sentences to the correct letters in the picture.**

1. The girl **cuts** up a carrot. _____

2. The girl's mother **fries** the onions in a pan. _____

3. The onions **smell** delicious. _____

4. There are many kinds of **vegetables**. _____

5. The girl's grandmother is very **sick**. _____

6. The girl's mother knows a good soup **recipe**. _____

Think Together Look at the picture and check Yes, No, or Don't know.

	Yes	No	Don't know
1. The girl likes cooking with her mother.	☐	☐	☐
2. Vegetable soup is good for your health.	☐	☐	☐

Healthy Vegetable Soup

Karen's grandmother is sick in bed. So Karen's mom decides to cook delicious and healthy vegetable soup for her. Vegetable soup is Karen's favorite dish! She helps her mom to cook it. First they wash their hands. Then they cut up vegetables. Karen cuts up a potato, a carrot, and a pumpkin. Her mom cuts up onions and garlic. Then they heat some oil in a pan. They fry the onions and garlic, and then add the other vegetables. The vegetables become golden brown and soft. Next they add water, salt, and some spices. Now it smells delicious! Karen is happy to learn her mom's special recipe.

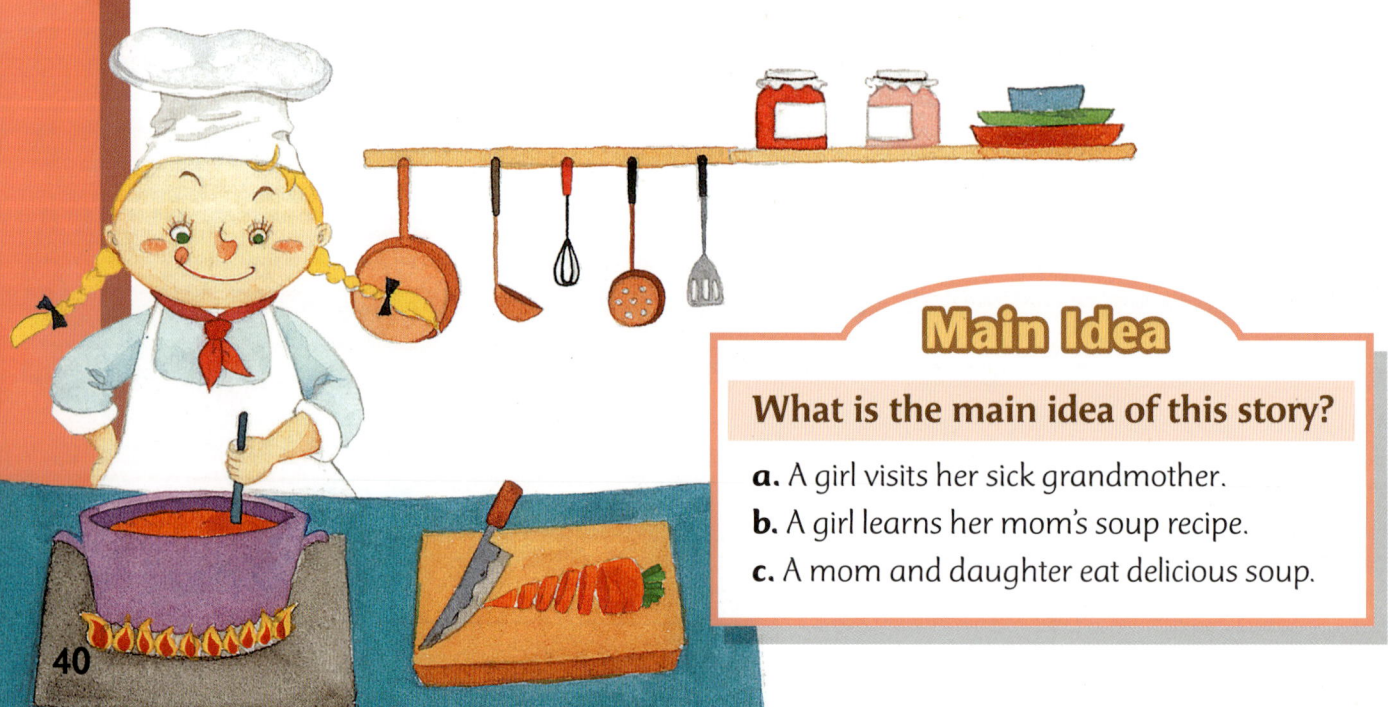

Main Idea

What is the main idea of this story?

a. A girl visits her sick grandmother.

b. A girl learns her mom's soup recipe.

c. A mom and daughter eat delicious soup.

40

◆ **Choose the best answer.** ....

1. Who do Karen and her mom make the soup for?

   a. Karen's father

   b. Karen's grandfather

   c. Karen's grandmother

2. What is the first thing Karen and her mom do?

   a. heat oil in a pan   b. cut up vegetables   c. wash their hands

3. What does Karen's mom cut up?

   a. onions and garlic   b. a potato and onions   c. a pumpkin and a carrot

4. What is NOT needed for the soup?

   a. salt   b. sugar   c. spices

Vocabulary Expansion

◆ **Write the correct word for each sentence.** ....

1. _____ some salt if you like.

2. We _____ English at school.

3. Eating _____ food is important.

4. They _____ to go to the movies.

5. My _____ movie is *Kung Fu Panda*.

6. Indian people use many _____ when they cook.

add   decided   favorite   healthy   learn   spices

Summary

Step 1 Read the sentences and number them in the correct order.

Karen and her mom wash their hands. ◯

They heat some oil in a pan. ◯

They add water, salt, and some spices. ◯

They cut up vegetables. ◯

They fry the onions, garlic, and then the other vegetables. ◯

Step 2 Complete the summary with the correct words.

Karen helps her mom make _____ for her sick grandmother. Before they start cooking, they wash their hands. Then they _____ up vegetables. They heat some _____ in a pan to _____ the vegetables. Last, they add _____, salt, and some spices. Now the soup is ready!

| cut | fry | oil | soup | water |

The Story of Chewing Gum

Build Your Vocabulary

◆ **Match the sentences to the correct letters in the picture.**

1. The girl **chews** gum. _____

2. The boy is **outside** of the building. _____

3. The chewing gum **sticks** to the boy's shoe. _____

4. There are many **flavors** of chewing gum. _____

5. The chewing gum is shaped like a **cube**. _____

6. The man **boils** something in the glass bottle. _____

Think Together **Look at the picture and check Yes, No, or Don't know.**

	Yes	No	Don't know
1. People like chewing gum because of its flavor.	☐	☐	☐
2. It is not very healthy to chew sugary gum.	☐	☐	☐

The Story of Chewing Gum

Chewing gum sticks to chairs, desks, shoes, and everything else. But most people love it! It was first made in 1869 by Thomas Adams. He was an inventor in New York. He boiled natural tree gum because he wanted to make it chewy. Then he added flavors. Later, in the 1880s, the Fleer brothers made cubes of gum. The gum had sugar on the outside. Sugary gum became popular. But it was bad for teeth. Then, in the 1960s, chewing gum companies introduced sugar-free gum. Today there are many kinds of sugar-free chewing gum. And there are many flavors, from mint to vanilla to cola.

Main Idea

What is the main idea of this text?

a. facts about the history of chewing gum
b. reasons why chewing gum is so popular
c. a story about the inventor of chewing gum

◆ **Choose the best answer.**

1. When did Thomas Adams invent chewing gum?

    a. in 1869   b. in 1880   c. in 1960

2. What kind of gum did the Fleer brothers make?

    a. sugary gum   b. sugarless gum   c. gum with flavors

3. What was the problem with sugary gum?

    a. It had a bad taste.

    b. It was bad for teeth.

    c. It was too hard to chew.

4. What is NOT true about sugar-free gum?

    a. It is not chewy.

    b. There are many kinds of it.

    c. It was first made in the 1960s.

Vocabulary Expansion

◆ **Write the correct word for each sentence.**

1. I brush my _____ after lunch.

2. He doesn't like _____ snacks.

3. My mother works at a car _____.

4. She knows _____ about basketball.

5. The teacher _____ a new student to the class.

6. Alexander Bell was the _____ of the telephone.

> company   everything   introduced   inventor   sugary   teeth

Summary

Step 1 Complete the chart with the correct words.

The Story of Chewing Gum

In 1869		In the 1880s		In the 1960s
Thomas Adams _____ tree gum to make it _____ .	→	The Fleer brothers made _____ of _____ chewing gum.	→	Chewing gum _____ made sugar-free gum.

boiled   chewy   companies   cubes   sugary

Step 2 Complete the summary with the correct words.

Chewing gum was first made in 1869 by Thomas Adams. He boiled _____ tree gum and _____ flavors. In the 1880s, the Fleer brothers made cubes of sugary gum. It was very _____ but bad for teeth. In the 1960s, companies introduced _____ gum. Now there are many kinds and _____ of sugar-free gum.

added   flavors   natural   popular   sugar-free

46

Pizza Tag

Build Your Vocabulary

◆ **Match the sentences to the correct letters in the picture.**

1. The children play in the **backyard**. _____

2. The boy **tags** a girl. _____

3. The boy's mother is **inside** the house. _____

4. The mother **calls out** to the children. _____

5. There are many **toppings** on the pizza. _____

6. There are **mushrooms** under the tree. _____

Think Together **Look at the picture and check Yes, No, or Don't know.**

	Yes	No	Don't know
1. The children are playing hide-and-seek.	☐	☐	☐
2. Playing outside is always fun.	☐	☐	☐

Pizza Tag

Sam is playing in the backyard with his friends. They are playing "pizza tag." Sam is the "chef." The chef tags the other kids and calls out a pizza topping. "Mushrooms!" yells Sam as he tags Andy. "Mushrooms!" repeats Andy. Then Sam tags Naomi. "Pineapple!" he yells. "Mushrooms and pineapple!" repeats Naomi. Then Sam tags Mike. "Bacon!" says Sam. "Mushrooms, pineapple, and bacon," repeats Mike. Soon the list of toppings gets longer and longer! When Sam tags Jenny, she can't remember all the toppings. So, she becomes the chef. After some time, the kids get hungry. "Come inside," calls Sam's mom. She made pizza for them—with all the toppings.

Main Idea

What is the main idea of this story?

a. making pizza tag rules
b. playing pizza tag outside
c. making pizza with friends

48

Comprehension

◆ **Choose the best answer.** ....

1. Who is the first chef?

    a. Sam   b. Andy   c. Jenny

2. Who can't remember all the pizza toppings?

    a. Mike   b. Naomi   c. Jenny

3. What happens if you can't remember all the toppings?

    a. You are out.

    b. You make pizza.

    c. You become the chef.

4. What is NOT part of pizza tag?

    a. tagging another person

    b. finding the list of toppings

    c. repeating the pizza toppings

Vocabulary Expansion

◆ **Write the correct word for each sentence.** ....

1. _____ this sentence after me.

2. The TV show is about a famous _____.

3. I know her, but I can't _____ her name.

4. He was a dancer before he _____ a singer.

5. My mother always makes a shopping _____.

6. Two boys _____ at each other on the street.

| became | chef | list | remember | repeat | yell |

Summary

Step 1 Complete the chart with the correct words.

Pizza Tag

Sam	**Andy, Naomi, and Mike**	**Jenny**
tags the _____ kids and _____ a pizza topping	_____ all the pizza toppings when the _____ tags them	can't remember all the toppings and _____ the chef

becomes   calls out   chef   other   repeat

Step 2 Complete the summary with the correct words.

Sam and his friends are playing "pizza tag" in the _____.
Sam is the "chef," so he _____ the other kids and calls
out pizza _____. Andy, Naomi, and Mike _____
all the toppings. But Jenny can't remember them all, so she
becomes the chef. After the game, Sam's mom calls
_____ in for pizza.

backyard   everyone   remember   tags   toppings

Flight of the Gibbon

Build Your Vocabulary

◆ **Match the sentences to the correct letters in the picture.**

1. The boy **puts on** a helmet. _____

2. The man climbs the **ladder**. _____

3. The woman moves along the **rope**. _____

4. The floors are high **above** the ground. _____

5. The gibbon moves **between** the trees. _____

6. The **staff** member helps the boy. _____

Think Together Look at the picture and check Yes, No, or Don't know.

	Yes	No	Don't know
1. The boy on the floor looks scared.	☐	☐	☐
2. It looks like fun to slide along the rope.	☐	☐	☐

Flight of the Gibbon

Do you want to fly through the treetops? Now you can! Flight of the Gibbon is an adventure activity for nature lovers. With ropes and ladders, you can go from tree to tree just like a gibbon. Before you start the adventure, you put on safety clothing and a helmet. Then friendly staff members take you into the rainforest. There are wooden floors high in the trees. And there are ropes between the trees. You slide along the ropes at high speeds. At times, you are 100 meters above the ground! But don't worry–it's safe. And you can enjoy the sights and sounds of the jungle while you play.

Main Idea

What is the main idea of this text?

a. introducing an exciting activity
b. introducing gibbons in the jungle
c. introducing plants in the rainforest

Comprehension

◆ **Choose the best answer.** ....

1. Who will enjoy Flight of the Gibbon the most?

    a. nature lovers   b. sports fans   c. animal owners

2. How do you go from tree to tree?

    a. climbing up ropes   b. sliding along ropes   c. jumping onto the floors

3. Where can you enjoy Flight of the Gibbon?

    a. at the zoo   b. in the rainforest   c. at a theme park

4. What is NOT true about Flight of the Gibbon?

    a. People put on safety clothing and a helmet.

    b. The staff members hold the rope for people.

    c. People can be 100 meters above the ground.

Vocabulary Expansion

◆ **Write the correct word for each sentence.** ....

1. We need to protect _____.

2. Are you ready for a new _____?

3. Wear your _____ when you ride a bike.

4. Children learn about school _____ rules.

5. Let's enjoy the wonderful _____ of the city.

6. Mr. Smith is a(n) _____ man in my neighborhood.

adventure   friendly   helmet   nature   safety   sights

Summary

Step 1 Complete the chart with the correct words.

How to Enjoy Flight of the Gibbon

1. Put on _____ clothing and a helmet.

2. Follow _____ members into the rainforest.

3. _____ the ladder to the wooden floors.

4. Slide along the _____ between the trees.

5. Enjoy the sights and sounds of the _____.

climb   jungle   ropes   safety   staff

Step 2 Complete the summary with the correct words.

Flight of the Gibbon is an exciting _____ for nature lovers. You can go from tree to tree with ropes and _____. First, you put on safety clothing and a(n) _____ and go into the _____. You climb up to the floors high in the trees. Then you _____ fast along the ropes between the trees while you enjoy the sights and sounds of the jungle.

adventure   helmet   ladders   rainforest   slide

Fun in Science Class

Build Your Vocabulary

◆ **Match the sentences to the correct letters in the picture.**

1. The girl's piece of paper is **flat**. _____

2. The blackboard is very **large**. _____

3. The children wear the **same** shoes. _____

4. The boy **pushes** the teacher's desk. _____

5. The teacher thinks about a **parachute**. _____

6. Two pieces of paper **fall** to the ground. _____

Think Together **Look at the picture and check Yes, No, or Don't know.**

	Yes	No	Don't know
1. Two pieces of paper fall at the same speed.	☐	☐	☐
2. A parachute falls quickly to the ground.	☐	☐	☐

Fun in Science Class

"Let's do an experiment," says Ms. Adams, the science teacher. She asks Mindy and Robert to help her. She gives a ball of paper to Robert. Then she gives a flat piece of paper to Mindy. "Now, drop them," she says. At the same time, Mindy and Robert drop their pieces of paper. Robert's paper ball falls quickly to the ground. But Mindy's flat piece of paper falls down slowly. Why does it happen? Ms. Adams explains, "Mindy's paper is large and flat, so more air is under it. Because more air pushes up under it, it falls more slowly." Mindy says, "It's just like a parachute!" "Right!" says Ms. Adams.

Main Idea

What is the main idea of this story?

a. doing a paper experiment in class
b. throwing and catching paper balls
c. learning about the shapes of paper

Comprehension

◆ **Choose the best answer.**

1. Who drops the ball of paper?

    a. Robert   b. Mindy   c. Ms. Adams

2. What is true about the experiment?

    a. Mindy's paper falls more quickly.

    b. Robert's paper falls more quickly.

    c. Both of their pieces of paper fall at the same time.

3. What is the flat piece of paper like?

    a. a ball   b. a ship   c. a parachute

4. Why do parachutes fall slowly?

    a. because air goes beside them

    b. because air moves around them

    c. because air pushes up under them

Vocabulary Expansion

◆ **Write the correct word for each sentence.**

1. He walks very _____.

2. The girl is sitting _____ a tree.

3. A funny thing _____ yesterday.

4. He tried to _____ the situation.

5. We don't have _____ class today.

6. The Wright brothers did a simple _____ with kites.

> experiment   explain   happened   quickly   science   under

Step 1 Complete the chart with the correct words.

Falling Paper Experiment

Robert's Paper

· a round _____ of paper

· falls _____

Mindy's Paper

· a _____ piece of paper

· falls _____

· _____ air _____ up under the paper

| ball | flat | more | pushes | quickly | slowly |

Step 2 Complete the summary with the correct words.

Mindy and Robert help Ms. Adams with a science _____. Robert drops a ball of paper and Mindy drops a flat _____ of paper. Robert's ball of paper falls quickly, but Mindy's flat piece of paper falls _____. It is because more air pushes up _____ Mindy's paper. So it falls slowly like a _____.

| experiment | parachute | piece | slowly | under |

Homemade Volcano

Build Your Vocabulary

◆ **Match the sentences to the correct letters in the picture.**

1. The **bottles** are empty. _____

2. The **dough** is in a bowl. _____

3. There is **detergent** on the counter. _____

4. The girl and the boy make a **volcano** on the table. _____

5. The girl **pours** something into the hole. _____

6. The **lava** comes out of the volcano in the picture. _____

Think Together Look at the picture and check Yes, No, or Don't know.

	Yes	No	Don't know
1. The lava from the volcano is very hot.	☐	☐	☐
2. The children are cooking in the kitchen.	☐	☐	☐

Homemade Volcano

Do you want to try a fun science experiment at home? Then make your own volcano! First, make some dough. Mix six cups of flour, two cups of salt, and two cups of water in a bowl. Use your hands to make the dough. Next, stand a plastic soda bottle in a pan. Put the dough around the bottle in a volcano shape. Then pour warm water into the bottle. Add red food coloring to make the lava red. Then, add a few drops of detergent and two tablespoons of baking soda. Finally, get some vinegar and slowly pour it into the bottle. Watch out! Here comes the lava!

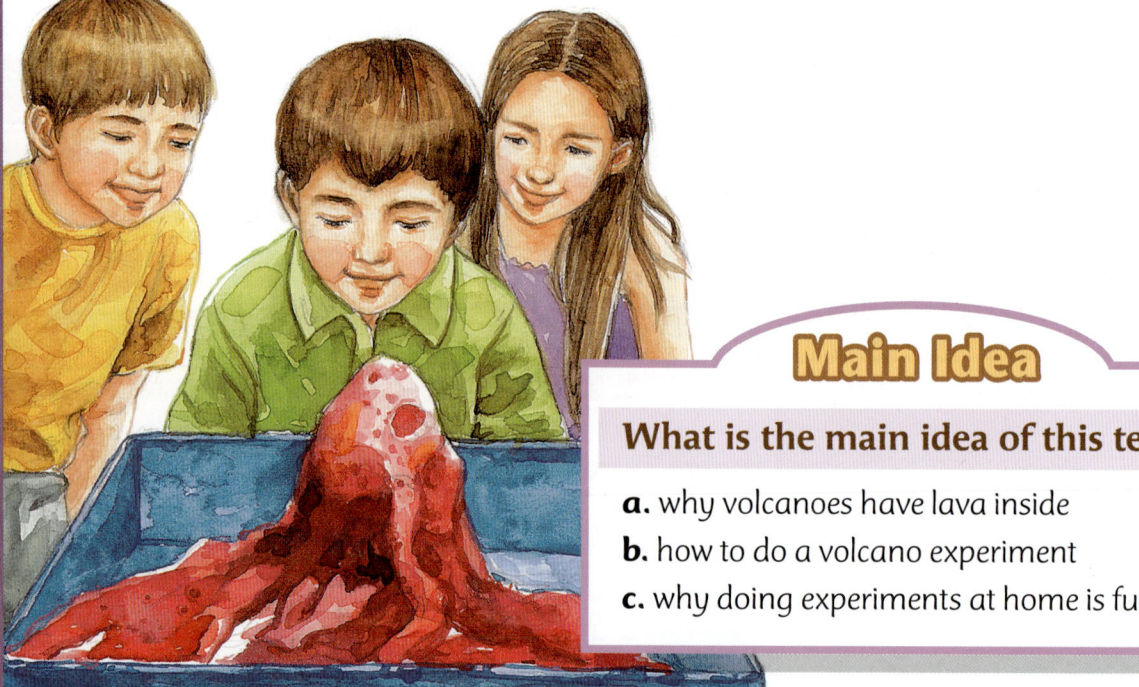

Main Idea

What is the main idea of this text?

a. why volcanoes have lava inside
b. how to do a volcano experiment
c. why doing experiments at home is fun

Comprehension

◆ **Choose the best answer.** ....

1. What is the first step of the experiment?

    a. making dough   b. adding detergent   c. pouring warm water

2. Where do you put the soda bottle?

    a. in a pan   b. in the sink   c. on the table

3. What do you add to make the lava red?

    a. vinegar   b. detergent   c. food coloring

4. What happens when you pour vinegar into the bottle?

    a. The lava comes out.

    b. The water gets warm.

    c. The dough becomes soft.

Vocabulary Expansion

◆ **Write the correct word for each sentence.** ....

1. _____ smells very sour.

2. Oil and water don't _____.

3. He is wearing a _____ jacket.

4. These toys are made of _____.

5. You need _____ to make bread.

6. Draw a star _____ and cut it out.

| flour | mix | plastic | shape | vinegar | warm |

Summary

Step 1 Read the sentences and number them in the correct order.

Make some dough with flour, salt, and water. ◯

Pour vinegar into the bottle. ◯

Add red food coloring, detergent, and baking soda. ◯

Pour warm water into the bottle. ◯

Put the dough around a bottle. ◯

Step 2 Complete the summary with the correct words.

You can make your own _____ at home. First, make _____. Next, make a volcano shape by putting the dough around a plastic soda bottle. Then pour _____ water with red food coloring into the bottle. Also, add detergent and baking soda. Finally, pour _____ into the bottle to make the _____ come.

| dough | lava | vinegar | volcano | warm |

The Zebra and the Baboon

Build Your Vocabulary

◆ **Match the sentences to the correct letters in the picture.**

1. The baboon has brown **fur**.   _____

2. The zebra has black and white **stripes**.   _____

3. The baboon has a red **bottom**.   _____

4. The zebra looks **angry**.   _____

5. The zebra **kicks** in the air.   _____

6. The monkey **guards** his family.   _____

Think Together **Look at the picture and check Yes, No, or Don't know.**

	Yes	No	Don't know
1. The zebra and the baboon are friends.	☐	☐	☐
2. The animals all want to drink some water.	☐	☐	☐

The Zebra and the Baboon

Long ago, there was a selfish baboon. He guarded a waterhole, so other animals couldn't drink there. He even built a fire and guarded the waterhole at night. One day, a zebra arrived. Back then, the zebra had white fur without stripes. As he came near, the baboon jumped up. "Go away!" he said. The zebra was angry. "This water is for everyone," he yelled. They started to fight. Suddenly, the zebra kicked the baboon hard. They both fell into the baboon's fire. The zebra burned his fur and the baboon burned his bottom. That's why the zebra has black stripes and the baboon has a red bottom.

Main Idea

What is the main idea of this story?

a. how the zebra and the baboon got their looks

b. how the zebra and the baboon became close friends

c. why the zebra and the baboon fought with other animals

◆ **Choose the best answer.** ....

1. What did the baboon guard?

   a. a fire   b. a house   c. a waterhole

2. Why was the zebra angry?

   a. because the baboon hit him hard

   b. because the zebra burned his fur

   c. because the baboon didn't share the water

3. During the fight, what did the zebra do?

   a. He made a fire.   b. He asked for help.   c. He kicked the baboon.

4. What happened to the baboon in the end?

   a. He fell into the waterhole.

   b. He burned his bottom in the fire.

   c. He burned his fur and got stripes.

Vocabulary Expansion

◆ **Write the correct word for each sentence.** ....

1. The train _____ a little late.

2. Many soldiers _____ in the war.

3. _____ my sister and I love milk.

4. _____ people don't care about others.

5. They _____ a new house near the park.

6. My little sister can't sleep _____ her doll.

| arrived | both | built | fought | selfish | without |

Summary

Step 1 Complete the chart with the correct words.

The Zebra and the Baboon's Fight

Baboon built a fire and guarded a _____ from everyone

Zebra was _____ and wanted the baboon to share water with others

Fight

Baboon burned his _____ and got a _____ bottom

Zebra burned his _____ and got _____ stripes

angry   black   bottom   fur   red   waterhole

Step 2 Complete the summary with the correct words.

Long ago, a _____ baboon guarded a waterhole. He built a _____ and guarded it at night. One day, a zebra with _____ fur and no stripes came and wanted water. But the baboon yelled at him to go away. They _____ and fell into the fire. The zebra _____ his fur and got black stripes. And the baboon got a red bottom.

burned   fire   fought   selfish   white

66

A Special Lion, Little Tyke

Build Your Vocabulary

◆ **Match the sentences to the correct letters in the picture.**

1. A young lion is called a **cub**. _____

2. The big lion **attacks** the cub. _____

3. The woman gives **meat** to the lion. _____

4. The lion **throws up** on the floor. _____

5. The **lamb** looks at the lion. _____

6. The woman and the animals are on a **farm**. _____

Think Together Look at the picture and check Yes, No, or Don't know.

	Yes	No	Don't know
1. The other animals are afraid of the lion.	☐	☐	☐
2. Lions only eat meat.	☐	☐	☐

A Special Lion, Little Tyke

L ittle Tyke was a lion cub. She was born at a zoo in Washington, U.S.A., in 1946. Sadly, her mother attacked her when she was born. So, a married couple took her to their farm. When she was three months old, the couple gave her some meat. But Little Tyke threw up. She didn't even drink milk mixed with beef blood. Usually, lions love to eat lots of meat. But Little Tyke was different. She didn't want to have meat. She even made friends with other animals. Her best friend was a lamb called Becky. The two animals played together their whole lives.

Main Idea

What is the main idea of this text?

a. Little Tyke didn't like to live in a zoo.
b. Little Tyke loved to play with people.
c. Little Tyke was different from other lions.

Comprehension

◆ **Choose the best answer.** ....

1. Why did Little Tyke leave the zoo?

    a. because her mother died

    b. because she hurt another cub

    c. because her mother attacked her

2. What do lions usually love to eat?

    a. milk   b. meat   c. beef blood

3. What happened when the couple gave Little Tyke meat?

    a. She ate it all.   b. She threw up.   c. She attacked them.

4. Who was Little Tyke's best friend on the farm?

    a. a lamb   b. another lion   c. a girl called Becky

Vocabulary Expansion

◆ **Write the correct word for each sentence.** ....

1. My favorite _____ is May.

2. The hospital needs lots of _____.

3. He can speak five _____ languages.

4. They ate _____ and salad for dinner.

5. He spent the _____ weekend sleeping.

6. I saw monkeys at the _____ yesterday.

| beef | blood | different | month | whole | zoo |

Summary

Step 1 Complete the chart with the correct words.

Little Tyke

was born at a _____ in Washington in 1946

was attacked by her mother and moved to a _____

didn't want any _____ or beef _____

made _____ with other _____

animals   blood   farm   friends   meat   zoo

Step 2 Complete the summary with the correct words.

Little Tyke was _____ in a Washington zoo in 1946.
But when she was born, her mother _____ her. So a
married _____ took her to their farm. They gave Little
Tyke some meat one day, but she just _____. Little
Tyke was _____ from other lions. She didn't want any
meat. She even made friends with other animals.

attacked   born   couple   different   threw up

Heroes with Parachutes

Build Your Vocabulary

◆ **Match the sentences to the correct letters in the picture.**

1. There are many trees in the **forest**. _____

2. The trees are **burning**. _____

3. The firefighters carry heavy **equipment** with them. _____

4. The firefighter **puts out** the fire. _____

5. A **brave** firefighter goes into the burning forest. _____

6. Jumping from a plane looks **scary**. _____

Think Together Look at the picture and check Yes, No, or Don't know.

	Yes	No	Don't know
1. The firefighters are not afraid of fire.	☐	☐	☐
2. It is not easy to put out forest fires.	☐	☐	☐

Heroes with Parachutes

C an you imagine jumping from a plane into a burning forest? It's a usual day's work for smokejumpers! Smokejumpers are special firefighters. They put out dangerous forest fires. Today I watched a TV show about smokejumpers. On the TV show, the big forest fires looked really scary. But the smokejumpers were very brave. To get to the fires, they wear parachutes and jump from planes. Smokejumpers carry around 50 kg of equipment with them, so they are healthy and strong. They stay calm when they are working. Sometimes, smokejumpers spend up to five days fighting forest fires. I think they are heroes!

Main Idea

What is the main idea of this story?

a. studying about smokejumpers in class
b. reading a book about dangerous forest fires
c. watching a TV show about special firefighters

◆ **Choose the best answer.** ....

1. What kind of fires do smokejumpers put out?

   a. house fires   b. forest fires   c. airplane fires

2. How do smokejumpers get to the burning fires?

   a. on foot   b. by parachute   c. by fire truck

3. What does NOT describe smokejumpers?

   a. scared of fires   b. healthy and strong   c. calm when working

4. What does the writer think about smokejumpers?

   a. They are good friends.
   b. They are brave heroes.
   c. They are helpful workers.

Vocabulary Expansion

◆ **Write the correct word for each sentence.** ....

1. It was _____ in the library.

2. The old bridge looks really _____.

3. I _____ a lot of time watching TV.

4. Can you _____ a world without light?

5. The soldier became a _____ after the war.

6. The _____ saved a family from a house fire.

> calm   dangerous   firefighters   hero   imagine   spend

Summary

Step 1 Complete the chart with the correct words.

Smokejumpers

- put out dangerous _____ fires
- jump from planes with _____
- carry heavy _____
- stay _____ when working
- _____ many days fighting forest fires

calm   equipment   forest   spend   parachutes

Step 2 Complete the summary with the correct words.

Today I watched a TV show about smokejumpers. They are special _____. They jump from planes with parachutes and _____ dangerous forest fires. Smokejumpers _____ heavy equipment, so they are healthy and strong. They stay calm when they are _____ fires. I think smokejumpers are _____.

carry   fighting   firefighters   heroes   put out

A Smart Star

Build Your Vocabulary

◆ **Match the sentences to the correct letters in the picture.**

1. There are **several** cameras. _____

2. The **actress** smiles for the cameras. _____

3. The actress wins an **award**. _____

4. The people look at the **famous** actress. _____

5. The **young** girl is with her father. _____

6. The actress thinks about her **exam**. _____

Think Together **Look at the picture and check Yes, No, or Don't know.**

	Yes	No	Don't know
1. The actress is a smart student.	☐	☐	☐
2. The people are fans of the actress.	☐	☐	☐

A Smart Star

If you like the *Star Wars* movies, then you will know about Natalie Portman. She played a queen in the movies. Natalie Portman started acting when she was young. She was only 13 when she appeared in her first movie, *Leon*. After she was in the *Star Wars* movies, she became famous. Also, she won several awards as an actress. But she still studied hard at school. She didn't even go to see the first showing of her *Star Wars* movie. Instead, she studied for her exams! Later, Portman went to Harvard University. "College is more important than acting," she said. "Being smart is better than being a movie star."

Main Idea

What is the main idea of this text?

a. Natalie Portman went to a good school.

b. Natalie Portman is a famous and smart actress.

c. Natalie Portman stopped studying to become an actress.

Comprehension

◆ **Choose the best answer.** ....

1. When did Natalie Portman become famous?

   a. after *Leon*   b. after *Star Wars*   c. before *Star Wars*

2. Why was Natalie Portman NOT at the first showing of her *Star Wars* movie?

   a. because she was studying
   b. because she was too young
   c. because she was filming another movie

3. What was more important to Natalie Portman than making movies?

   a. being happy   b. being beautiful   c. being smart

4. What is NOT true about Natalie Portman?

   a. She started acting at 13.
   b. She won some awards at school.
   c. She studied at Harvard University.

Vocabulary Expansion

◆ **Write the correct word for each sentence.** ....

1. I visited my sister's _____.

2. The monkey is a _____ animal.

3. Spain _____ the World Cup in 2010.

4. The man suddenly _____ in the room.

5. I met a movie star for the _____ time.

6. She had no honey, so she used sugar _____.

> appeared   college   first   instead   smart   won

Step 1 Complete the chart with the correct words.

Natalie Portman

As an Actress
· appeared in her _____ movie, *Leon*, at 13
· became _____ after the *Star Wars* movies
· won several _____

As a Student
· studied _____ at school
· went to Harvard _____

| awards | famous | first | hard | University |

Step 2 Complete the summary with the correct words.

Natalie Portman _____ in her first movie, *Leon*, at 13. After the *Star Wars* movies, she became famous and _____ several awards. But she still studied hard at school. She didn't even see the first _____ of her *Star Wars* movie. She studied for her _____ instead. Later she _____ to Harvard University.

| appeared | exams | showing | went | won |

Who Did It?

Build Your Vocabulary

◆ **Match the sentences to the correct letters in the picture.**

1. There is a **mall** on the main street. _____

2. The road is **wide**. _____

3. The street between the buildings is **narrow**. _____

4. The **principal** talks to the girl. _____

5. The girl looks at the **footprints**. _____

6. There is no one on the **sidewalk**. _____

Think Together **Look at the picture and check Yes, No, or Don't know.**

	Yes	No	Don't know
1. The principal looks worried.	☐	☐	☐
2. The girl knows who left the footprints.	☐	☐	☐

Who Did It?

Last Saturday, I met Rachel, Sara, and Tina at the mall. Rachel showed me her new shoes. They were very wide. Poor Sara had a broken leg. So, she couldn't walk fast. Tina said, "Let's have some ice cream together, Amy." But I wanted to go home. On my way home, I saw the school principal outside the school. He was looking at the sidewalk. He was angry. "Somebody jumped in this wet cement!" he said. I saw two narrow footprints there. "Who did it?" I asked. "I don't know. I only saw Rachel, Sara, and Tina here earlier," he said. Then I knew who did it.

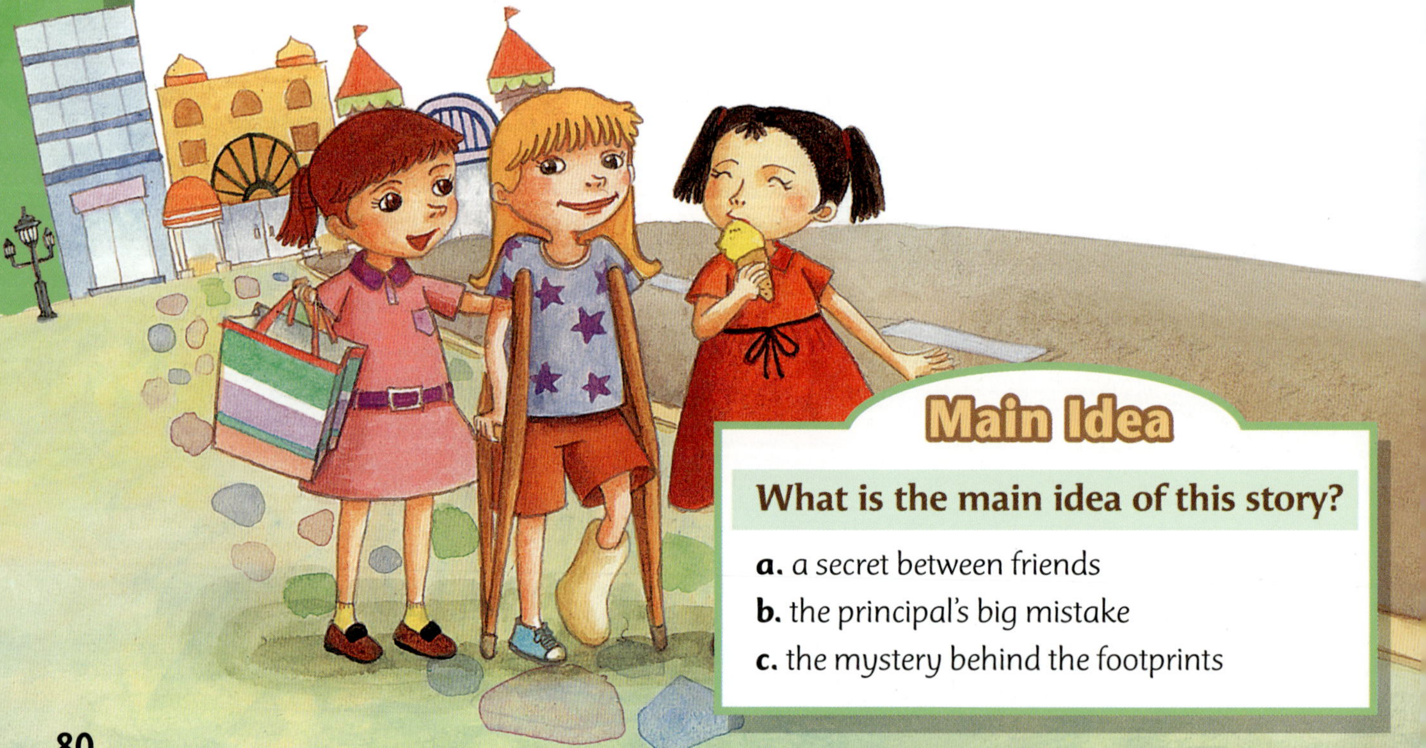

Main Idea

What is the main idea of this story?

a. a secret between friends
b. the principal's big mistake
c. the mystery behind the footprints

Comprehension

◆ **Choose the best answer.**

1. Where did Amy meet her three friends?

a. at school   b. at the mall   c. on the sidewalk

2. What did Rachel have?

a. new shoes   b. ice cream   c. a broken leg

3. Why was the principal angry?

a. because somebody took his shoes

b. because somebody jumped in the wet cement

c. because somebody left their shoes in the cement

4. What is NOT true about the story?

a. Amy didn't eat ice cream with the girls.

b. Amy saw who jumped in the wet cement.

c. The principal saw three girls on the street.

Vocabulary Expansion

◆ **Write the correct word for each sentence.**

1. _____ took my bag!

2. When did you _____ Jake?

3. Our school has _____ walls.

4. I went to bed _____ last night.

5. I want to _____ you my new pet.

6. The ground was _____ after the rain.

cement   early   meet   show   somebody   wet

Summary

Step 1 Complete the chart with the correct words.

> **Mystery** Who left footprints in the wet cement?

> **Clue 1** Amy met three girls at the mall.
> - Rachel had very _____ new shoes.
> - Sara had a broken _____.
> - Tina wanted to eat _____.
>
> **Clue 2** The _____ saw three girls near the school.
>
> **Clue 3** Somebody _____ in the cement.
>
> **Clue 4** The footprints in the cement are _____.

*The footprints are Tina's!

> ice cream   jumped   leg   narrow   principal   wide

Step 2 Complete the summary with the correct words.

> I met three friends at the _____. Rachel had new shoes.
> They were wide. Sara had a _____ leg. Tina wanted to
> eat ice cream, but I went home. Outside my school, I saw the
> principal. He was _____ because of two narrow
> _____ in the wet cement. He said only Rachel, Sara, and
> Tina were there _____. Then I knew who did it.
>
> > angry   broken   earlier   footprints   mall

82

The Famous Sherlock Holmes

Build Your Vocabulary

◆ Match the sentences to the correct letters in the picture.

1. The writer **creates** a story. _____

2. The writer **smokes** a pipe. _____

3. The **thin** man is wearing a long coat. _____

4. The men are wearing **hats**. _____

5. The **British** flag is on the wall. _____

6. Somebody **visits** the man's house. _____

Think Together Look at the picture and check Yes, No, or Don't know.

	Yes	No	Don't know
1. The man in the middle is looking for something.	☐	☐	☐
2. The man outside of the house needs some help.	☐	☐	☐

The Famous Sherlock Holmes

Sherlock Holmes is a British detective. There are many books, TV shows, plays, and movies about him. People around the world love him. Although he is very famous, he is not a real person. However, in a newspaper story, 21 percent of British people thought he was real! Arthur Conan Doyle created Sherlock Holmes in 1887. Holmes is tall and thin. He often wears a hunting hat and smokes a pipe. He lives with his friend Watson at 221b Baker Street, London. Watson helps Holmes solve mysteries. Today, fans of Sherlock Holmes can visit the Sherlock Holmes Museum. Where is it? It's at 221b Baker Street, London!

Main Idea

What is the main idea of this text?

a. Arthur Conan Doyle created Sherlock Holmes.

b. Sherlock Holmes is a famous detective character.

c. People around the world visit the Sherlock Holmes Museum.

Comprehension

◆ Choose the best answer. ....

1. What does Sherlock Holmes NOT have?

    a. a pipe   b. glasses   c. a hunting hat

2. Who is Watson?

    a. Holmes's friend   b. Holmes's boss   c. Holmes's brother

3. What is true about Sherlock Holmes?

    a. He appeared in a book in 1887.

    b. Most people believed he was real.

    c. He helped Watson solve mysteries.

4. What can you find at 221b Baker Street, London today?

    a. the Sherlock Holmes Museum

    b. the Arthur Conan Doyle Center

    c. the real home of Holmes and Watson

Vocabulary Expansion

◆ Write the correct word for each sentence. ....

1. Are these _____ flowers?

2. My sister works at an art _____.

3. She loves to read _____ stories.

4. I can't _____ this math problem.

5. Only 20 _____ of the students know the answer.

6. I enjoyed the _____ because the story was good.

    detective   museum   percent   play   real   solve

Step 1 Complete the chart with the correct words.

is a British _____ character

is tall and _____

Sherlock Holmes

wears a _____ hat and smokes a _____

lives in _____ with _____

detective   hunting   London   pipe   thin   Watson

Step 2 Complete the summary with the correct words.

Sherlock Holmes is a(n) _____ British detective. Arthur Conan Doyle created the _____ in 1887. Holmes is tall and thin. He has a hunting hat and a pipe. He and his _____ Watson live at 221b Baker Street, London. Today, that _____ is the place of the Sherlock Holmes _____.

address   character   famous   friend   Museum

Vocabulary List

Unit 1

poster
draw
excited
Native American
Mexican
Dutch
Indian
already
delicious
idea
bowl
perfect

Unit 2

special
elementary school
fun
regular
class
necklace
piece
cereal
picture
age
bring
stamp

Unit 3

birdhouse
wood
place
important
city

find
safe
nest
welcome
put
seed
call

Unit 4

kind
ground
cave
save
mud
wall
bathroom
roof
plenty of
natural
grow
plant

Unit 5

bad
library
choose
drop
carry
thank
forget
share
paint
shirt
wear
kind

Unit 6

bracelet
sign
friendship
popular
colorful
knot
pattern
mean
break
care
tradition
keep

Unit 7

cheerleader
active
fit
strong
practice
skill
jump
twist
move
rhythm
watch
proud

Unit 8

brush
player
slide
target
sweep

Northern
Championship
believe
fair
follow
rule
try

Unit 9

sick
decide
healthy
vegetable
favorite
cut
fry
add
spice
smell
learn
recipe

Unit 10

chew
stick
everything
inventor
boil
flavor
cube
outside
sugary
tooth
company
introduce

Unit 11

backyard
chef
tag
call out
topping
mushroom
yell
repeat
list
remember
become
inside

Unit 12

adventure
nature
rope
ladder
put on
safety
helmet
friendly
staff
between
above
sight

Unit 13

experiment
science
flat
same
fall

quickly
happen
explain
large
push
under
parachute

Unit 14

volcano
dough
mix
flour
plastic
bottle
shape
pour
warm
detergent
vinegar
lava

Unit 15

selfish
guard
build
arrive
fur
without
stripe
angry
fight
kick
both
bottom

Unit 16

cub
zoo
attack
farm
month
meat
throw up
beef
blood
different
lamb
whole

Unit 17

imagine
burn
forest
firefighter
put out
dangerous
scary
brave
equipment
calm
spend
hero

Unit 18

young
appear
first
famous
win

several
award
actress
instead
exam
college
smart

Unit 19

meet
mall
show
wide
principal
sidewalk
somebody
wet
cement
narrow
footprint
early

Unit 20

British
detective
play
percent
real
create
thin
hat
smoke
solve
visit
museum

Memo

Memo

LEVEL GUIDE NE_Build & Grow Products

Category	Level			Kindergarten (유치원)	Low Beginner (초등학교 1학년)	Beginner (초등학교 2학...)
	Books	Lexile®	Word Count			
Phonics	Phonics Show (Readers)					
	Come On, Phonics					
Readers	Show Time					
Coursebook	Come On, Everyone					
Reading	Read It! 30	BR~90L	30~45			
	Read It! 50	150L~240L	50~65			
	Read It! 100	270L~400L	70~100			
	Read It! 150	490L~640L	100~150			
	Read It! 200	660L~780L	160~220			
	Read It! 250	820L~920L	220~300			
	Reading Sketch	BR-300L	30~80			
	Reading Sponge	160L~280L	45~70			
	Read & Retell	240L~390L	50~80			
	Reading Sense	320L~410L	80~100			
	Reading Clue	490L~510L	100~130			
	The Basic Way	570L~660L	150~240			
	Read to Reach	600L~660L	140~220			
	Reading Source	580L~710L	140~200			
	The Best Way	860L~970L	230~340			
	Reading Peak	860L~900L	190~270			
	Read Up	1070L~1320L	350~500			
	Easy Link	BR~380L	20~80			
	Subject Link	430L~950L	90~360			
	Insight Link	400L~760L	80~250			
Listening	Listening Stage					
	Listening Seed					
	Listening Season					
	Listening Planner					
Writing	Write It!					
	Write Right					
Speaking	Everyone, Speak!					
Grammar	중학 영문법 Link					
	요즘 초등 영문법					
	Grammar Stage Starter					
	Grammar Stage					
	Grammar Stage Plus					
	Grammar Ten					
	Grammar Space					
	Grammar in Mind					
	Grammar in Focus					
	Grammar Effect					
Vocabulary	Word Up					
	요즘 초등 영단어					
Assessment	RADIX Reading for the TOEFL iBT Blue 1, 2 & Black 1, 2 Label		120~660			
	RADIX Listening for the TOEFL iBT Blue 1, 2 & Black 1, 2 Label		110~700			

Reading Clue

1

Workbook

NE_Build & Grow

Vocabulary Practice

A. Choose the best answer to complete the definition of each word.

1. If something is **delicious**, it _____ good.

   a. feels   b. sounds   c. tastes

2. To **draw** is to _____ a picture with a pen or pencil.

   a. sketch   b. take   c. watch

3. A **Dutch** person is from _____.

   a. Denmark   b. Germany   c. the Netherlands

4. If you **already** have something, you got it _____.

   a. before now   b. later   c. just now

5. A **bowl** is a round _____ that holds your food.

   a. bag   b. dish   c. spoon

6. If you are **excited**, you feel very _____.

   a. angry   b. happy   c. sad

B. Choose the best answer to complete each sentence.

1. I like (Mexican / Mexico) food a lot.

2. This dress is (correct / perfect) for me.

3. The (India / Indian) boy is eating curry.

4. Everyone liked her (idea / image) for the picnic.

5. The girl is putting a movie (poster / theater) on the wall.

6. The Native (America / American) woman is making a basket.

Sentence Practice

A. Unscramble the sentences.

1. (clogs / are / They / called).

⇨ _____

2. (a Mexican hat / He / draws).

⇨ _____

3. (draws / She / a big bowl / of Indian curry).

⇨ _____

4. (Please / something / from / draw / your country).

⇨ _____

B. Match the sentence parts.

1. Let's make   •   • a class poster.

2. She is   •   • she's hungry.

3. I think   •   • is perfect!

4. Now the poster   •   • Native American.

C. Translate each sentence into your language.

1. Anna draws a girl in a Native American dress.

⇨ _____

2. I want to draw an Indian dress, but the girl already has a dress.

⇨ _____

3. Why not give her some delicious food?

⇨ _____

Vocabulary Practice

A. Choose the best answer to complete the definition of each word.

1. A person's **age** is the _____ of years the person has lived.
   a. name   b. number   c. size

2. If something is **fun**, you _____ it.
   a. cook   b. enjoy   c. have

3. If you **bring** something, you _____ it to a place.
   a. send   b. want   c. take

4. A **picture** is a(n) _____ of someone or something.
   a. song   b. book   c. image

5. A **necklace** is a piece of jewelry that you _____ around your neck.
   a. see   b. touch   c. wear

6. A **stamp** is something you need when you _____ a letter.
   a. get   b. send   c. read

B. Choose the best answer to complete each sentence.

1. She already has seven (glasses / pieces) of candy.

2. I have (popular / special) plans for summer vacation.

3. (Strong / Regular) exercise is good for you.

4. I had a bowl of (cereal / steak) with milk for breakfast.

5. I am an (elementary / early) school student.

6. My first (class / school) begins at 9 o'clock in the morning.

Sentence Practice

A. Unscramble the sentences.

1. (a day / is / It / of fun and learning).

⇨ _____

2. (usually / The 100th day / is / in February).

⇨ _____

3. (on your 100th day / do you want / to bring / of school / What)?

⇨ _____

4. (for show and tell / They / to school / 100 special things / may bring).

⇨ _____

B. Match the sentence parts.

1. American schools •   • regular classes.

2. Students do not have •   • pictures of themselves at age 100.

3. They may draw •   • start in September.

4. The 100 things may be •   • photos, stamps, crayons, or anything!

C. Translate each sentence into your language.

1. The 100th day of school is a special day in elementary schools.

⇨ _____

2. They enjoy games and activities based on the number 100!

⇨ _____

3. They may make necklaces from 100 pieces of cereal.

⇨ _____

Vocabulary Practice

A. Choose the best answer to complete the definition of each word.

1. In a **city**, there are many people and _____.
   a. farms   b. rivers   c. buildings

2. A **nest** is a place where birds _____ and have babies.
   a. live   b. fly   c. carry

3. A **seed** is a small, hard thing from _____.
   a. meat   b. a bird   c. a plant

4. If you **find** something, you _____ what you are looking for.
   a. see   b. eat   c. show

5. **Wood** is the hard part of a _____.
   a. flower   b. book   c. tree

6. A **birdhouse** is a small _____ where birds can live.
   a. bowl   b. bag   c. box

B. Choose the best answer to complete each sentence.

1. The park is a nice (place / time) to visit.

2. I (hold / put) my backpack under my desk.

3. His family always (visits / welcomes) me to their home.

4. My name is Pamela, but you can (ask / call) me Pam.

5. My mom is the most (important / large) person in my life.

6. You should keep your money in a (hard / safe) place.

Sentence Practice

A. Unscramble the sentences.

1. (a place / has / It / for food and water).

⇨ _____

2. (out of / make / wood / the birdhouse / They).

⇨ _____

3. (even gives / a name / She / the birdhouse).

⇨ _____

4. (safe places / can't find / They / for their nests).

⇨ _____

B. Match the sentence parts.

1. Emily is making •

2. Emily's dad says •

3. Emily wants to •

4. This birdhouse is •

• a safe place.

• welcome many birds.

• that birdhouses are important.

• a birdhouse with her dad.

C. Translate each sentence into your language.

1. There aren't many birds in cities these days.

⇨ _____

2. Birds can live in the birdhouse and have babies.

⇨ _____

3. She puts seeds and fruits in the birdhouse.

⇨ _____

Vocabulary Practice

A. Choose the best answer to complete the definition of each word.

1. A **cave** is a large _____ in the side of a hill or under the ground.

    a. water   b. hole   c. rock

2. A **roof** is the cover or _____ of a building.

    a. floor   b. side   c. top

3. If something is **natural**, it was not made by _____.

    a. earth   b. nature   c. people

4. If you have **plenty of** time, you have _____ time.

    a. no   b. busy   c. a lot of

5. **Mud** is soft, _____ dirt on the ground.

    a. dry   b. small   c. wet

6. A **bathroom** is a room with a _____, a sink, and sometimes a shower.

    a. bed   b. toilet   c. table

B. Choose the best answer to complete each sentence.

1. They (grow / make) roses in their garden.

2. This (plant / rock) has long leaves.

3. What (kind / way) of tree is that?

4. There is a picture of my favorite singer on the (room / wall).

5. The leaves from the tree are falling to the (ground / sky).

6. You can (pay / save) energy by riding a bicycle.

Sentence Practice

A. Unscramble the sentences.

1. (grass / An earth house / on the roof / has).

⇨ _____

2. (natural light / through / comes in / Plenty of / the windows).

⇨ _____

3. (earth houses / in many ways / energy / It is because / can save).

⇨ _____

4. (mud walls / is built / An earth house / in the earth / and has).

⇨ _____

B. Match the sentence parts.

1. An earth house is • • earth houses?

2. Why do people build • • roof windows.

3. The bathroom has • • a new kind of home.

4. You can find it • • in Switzerland.

C. Translate each sentence into your language.

1. It is under the ground, so it looks like a cave or a fairy house.

⇨ _____

2. It stays warm in winter and cool in summer.

⇨ _____

3. You can grow many plants and pretty flowers there.

⇨ _____

Vocabulary Practice

A. Choose the best answer to complete the definition of each word.

1. If you **drop** something, you let it _____ down.
   a. fall   b. fly   c. put

2. If you **share** something, you use it _____ others.
   a. with   b. for   c. without

3. A **library** is a place where you can _____ and borrow books.
   a. buy   b. read   c. show

4. A **kind** person _____ others.
   a. helps   b. tells   c. uses

5. If you **carry** something, you _____ it from one place to another.
   a. buy   b. take   c. write

6. A **shirt** is a piece of clothing that covers the _____ body.
   a. lower   b. middle   c. upper

B. Choose the best answer to complete each sentence.

1. Don't (forget / remember) to turn off the TV.

2. I'd like to (tell / thank) you for the nice present.

3. I will (wear / wash) a raincoat if it rains a lot.

4. She (chose / cooked) a cheeseburger from the menu.

5. I had a (bad / good) dream last night, so I didn't sleep well.

6. I need blue and red (pants / paint) to make purple.

Sentence Practice

A. Unscramble the sentences.

1. (her / smiled / Tim / and thanked).

⇨ _____

2. (with me / can share / You / my lunch).

⇨ _____

3. (Tim / At lunch, / his bag / opened).

⇨ _____

4. (to wear / Luckily, / gave him / a soccer shirt / his friend Alex).

⇨ _____

B. Match the sentence parts.

1. At the school library,　•

2. It was too many　•

3. His friend Anita　•

4. She carried　•

•　and he dropped them.

•　some books for him.

•　Tim chose six books.

•　came over.

C. Translate each sentence into your language.

1. Yesterday, many bad things happened to Tim.

⇨ _____

2. Later, in art class, Tim got paint all over his T-shirt.

⇨ _____

3. Thanks to his kind friends, his bad day became a good day!

⇨ _____

Vocabulary Practice

A. Choose the best answer to complete the definition of each word.

1. If something is **colorful**, it has _____ different colors.

   a. few   b. dark   c. many

2. A **bracelet** is a band that you wear around your _____ .

   a. leg   b. wrist   c. neck

3. A **pattern** is a _____ that is repeated.

   a. design   b. plan   c. paper

4. A **knot** is made when you _____ something.

   a. cut   b. draw   c. tie

5. If you **keep** something, you don't _____ it or throw it away.

   a. have   b. lose   c. need

6. If something is **popular**, many people _____ it.

   a. put   b. like   c. forget

B. Choose the best answer to complete each sentence.

1. I know my friend Tom (cares / takes) for me.

2. A green light (means / stops) 'Go.'

3. He gave her a ring as a (show / sign) of his love.

4. I want to have a good (classmate / friendship) with you.

5. Be careful! The glass can (break / see) easily.

6. In the USA, watching fireworks is a 4th of July (tradition / place).

Sentence Practice

A. **Unscramble the sentences.**

1. (many knots / has / It / in different patterns).

⇨ _____

2. (true friendship / Its knots / that / cannot break / mean).

⇨ _____

3. (for your friend / a friendship bracelet / making / How about)?

⇨ _____

4. (a long time / takes / It / a bracelet / to make).

⇨ _____

B. **Match the sentence parts.**

1. A friendship bracelet is •   • and give it to your friend.

2. Do you want to keep •   • the bracelet until it breaks.

3. You make a bracelet •   • your best friend forever?

4. The friend wears •   • a special sign of friendship.

C. **Translate each sentence into your language.**

1. Today, giving a friendship bracelet is popular among teenagers.

⇨ _____

2. A friendship bracelet shows that you love and care for a special friend.

⇨ _____

3. In fact, it is a Native American tradition.

⇨ _____

Vocabulary Practice

A. Choose the best answer to complete the definition of each word.

1. If you **jump**, you move _____ into the air.

a. back   b. up   c. down

2. A **strong** person can lift _____ things.

a. heavy   b. hot   c. pretty

3. To **twist** something is to _____ it around.

a. break   b. cover   c. turn

4. A **cheerleader** cheers for a team at a _____.

a. test   b. picnic   c. sports event

5. If you **move**, you _____ position.

a. keep   b. know   c. change

6. If you **practice** something, you do it regularly to do it _____.

a. more   b. better   c. all the time

B. Choose the best answer to complete each sentence.

1. This music has a fast (rhythm / step).

2. He's very (happy / proud) of his daughter.

3. Your English (skills / ways) are great!

4. I am very (active / excited) and I like all kinds of sports.

5. The basketball player looks healthy and (fit / right).

6. I usually (watch / find) baseball games on Sundays.

Sentence Practice

A. Unscramble the sentences.

1. (run, jump, and twist / in the air / We).

⇨ _____

2. (so much / love / cheerleading / I)!

⇨ _____

3. (play football / Why / instead / can't you)?

⇨ _____

4. (cheerleading / you think / only for girls / Maybe / is).

⇨ _____

B. Match the sentence parts.

1. I felt • • so proud.

2. We practice • • our skills a lot.

3. Actually, cheerleading • • didn't like it.

4. At first, my dad • • is a very active sport.

C. Translate each sentence into your language.

1. Like other sports players, cheerleaders are fit and strong.

⇨ _____

2. Cheerleading is a team sport, so we learn to move together in rhythm.

⇨ _____

3. He watched me cheerleading at a football game.

⇨ _____

Vocabulary Practice

A. Choose the best answer to complete the definition of each word.

1. A **player** is someone who plays a _____ or sport.

    a. ball   b. movie   c. game

2. To **slide** is to make something move _____ on a surface.

    a. over   b. easily   c. up and down

3. If something is **northern**, it is in or _____ the north.

    a. from   b. out   c. under

4. If you **believe** in something, you think that it is _____.

    a. fun   b. right   c. popular

5. If you **sweep** the floor, you _____ dust or dirt from it.

    a. clean   b. put   c. walk

6. A **brush** is a thing made with a lot of hairs and a _____.

    a. handle   b. paint   c. paper

B. Choose the best answer to complete each sentence.

1. (Fair / Long) play is the most important thing.

2. You should hit the (shoot / target).

3. They (acted / followed) their captain's order.

4. I (do / try) to get up early these days.

5. Our team won the (champion / championship) game.

6. The player got a yellow card because he broke the (goals / rules).

Sentence Practice

A. **Unscramble the sentences.**

1. (is / a winter sport / It / called curling)!

⇨ _____

2. (move closer / the stones / to the target / helps / This).

⇨ _____

3. (always / They / the rules / follow).

⇨ _____

4. (cannot / with their brushes / Players / touch / the stones).

⇨ _____

B. **Match the sentence parts.**

1. Which sport has   •   • has eight stones.

2. Each team   •   • two teams of four players.

3. Curling has   •   • believe in fair play.

4. Curling players   •   • ice, big stones, and long brushes?

C. **Translate each sentence into your language.**

1. One player slides the stones to the target on the ice.

⇨ _____

2. The World Curling Championships are held each year.

⇨ _____

3. If you want to play a fun and unusual game, try curling!

⇨ _____

Unit 09 Healthy Vegetable Soup

Vocabulary Practice

A. Choose the best answer to complete the definition of each word.

1. A **vegetable** is part of a _____ that you can eat.
   a. flower   b. plant   c. seed

2. If you **fry** something, you cook it in hot _____.
   a. oil   b. water   c. sauce

3. To **add** is to _____ something with another thing.
   a. start   b. eat   c. put

4. Your **favorite** thing is the thing you _____ the most.
   a. need   b. like   c. see

5. If something is **healthy**, it is _____ for your body.
   a. good   b. salty   c. special

6. A **spice** is a powder or seed that you put in _____.
   a. food   b. bag   c. garden

B. Choose the best answer to complete each sentence.

1. Please (cut / make) the onion and put it in the pan.

2. This apple (smells / sounds) very sweet.

3. I want to (learn / try) how to play the cello.

4. He can't come to school today because he's (fit / sick).

5. I (decided / called) to go camping during summer vacation.

6. I found this (recipe / cooking) on the Internet.

18

Sentence Practice

A. Unscramble the sentences.

1. (her mom / it / to cook / helps / She).

⇨ _____

2. (their hands / they / wash / First).

⇨ _____

3. (is / Karen's grandmother / in bed / sick).

⇨ _____

4. (golden brown / become / and soft / The vegetables).

⇨ _____

B. Match the sentence parts.

1. Now it smells ●

2. Vegetable soup ●

3. They cut up ●

4. They heat ●

● vegetables.

● delicious!

● some oil in a pan.

● is Karen's favorite dish!

C. Translate each sentence into your language.

1. Karen's mom decides to cook delicious and healthy vegetable soup.

⇨ _____

2. They fry the onions and garlic, and then add the other vegetables.

⇨ _____

3. Karen is happy to learn her mom's special recipe.

⇨ _____

Vocabulary Practice

A. Choose the best answer to complete the definition of each word.

1. An **inventor** is a person who makes _____ things.

    a. good   b. new   c. strong

2. A **cube** is a thing with six _____ sides.

    a. circle   b. square   c. triangle

3. If you **boil** something, you cook it in hot _____.

    a. oil   b. water   c. salt

4. A **tooth** is one of the hard white things inside your _____.

    a. head   b. body   c. mouth

5. A **company** is a place where people make or _____ things.

    a. give   b. sell   c. take

6. **Flavor** is how food _____.

    a. tastes   b. looks   c. is cooked

B. Choose the best answer to complete each sentence.

1. You should not (chew / eat) gum in class.

2. The (out / outside) of the house looks beautiful.

3. This stamp doesn't (add / stick) to the postcard.

4. You can't buy (nothing / everything) you want.

5. (Spicy / Sugary) drinks like cola are bad for your health.

6. The company is (becoming / introducing) a new cell phone.

Sentence Practice

A. Unscramble the sentences.

1. (sugar / had / The gum / on the outside).

⇨ _____

2. (bad / Sugary gum / for teeth / was).

⇨ _____

3. (chewing gum / many kinds of / there are / Today / sugar-free).

⇨ _____

4. (Chewing gum / and everything else / chairs, desks, shoes, / sticks to).

⇨ _____

B. Match the sentence parts.

1. He was an inventor •   • in 1869 by Thomas Adams.

2. It was first made •   • made cubes of gum.

3. The Fleer brothers •   • became popular.

4. Sugary gum •   • in New York.

C. Translate each sentence into your language.

1. He boiled natural tree gum because he wanted to make it chewy.

⇨ _____

2. In the 1960s, chewing gum companies introduced sugar-free gum.

⇨ _____

3. There are many flavors, from mint to vanilla to cola.

⇨ _____

Vocabulary Practice

A. Choose the best answer to complete the definition of each word.

1. A **backyard** is a place _____ a house.

   a. behind   b. in front of   c. next to

2. A **topping** is something you put on top of _____ .

   a. box   b. building   c. food

3. A **chef** is someone who _____ food in a restaurant.

   a. eats   b. buys   c. cooks

4. A **list** is a set of _____ or items.

   a. books   b. clothes   c. names

5. If you **repeat** something, you say it _____ .

   a. again   b. quietly   c. slowly

6. If you **yell** something, you say it very _____ .

   a. loudly   b. quickly   c. sadly

B. Choose the best answer to complete each sentence.

1. If you need help, (call off / call out) my name.

2. I don't like the taste of (bedrooms / mushrooms).

3. To win this game, you must (run / tag) other players.

4. We went (inside / outside) because it was cold and raining.

5. I want to (become / change) good friends with you.

6. I am happy you (give / remember) me.

Sentence Practice

A. Unscramble the sentences.

1. (the kids / some time, / get / After / hungry).

⇨ _____

2. (She / for them / pizza / made / with all the toppings).

⇨ _____

3. (can't remember / all the toppings / Sam tags Jenny, / When / she).

⇨ _____

4. (the other kids / a pizza topping / and calls out / The chef / tags).

⇨ _____

B. Match the sentence parts.

1. They are playing •

2. "Mushrooms!" •

3. She becomes •

4. "Come inside," •

• "pizza tag."

• repeats Andy.

• calls Sam's mom.

• the chef.

C. Translate each sentence into your language.

1. Sam is playing in the backyard with his friends.

⇨ _____

2. "Mushrooms!" yells Sam as he tags Andy.

⇨ _____

3. Soon the list of toppings gets longer and longer!

⇨ _____

Vocabulary Practice

A. Choose the best answer to complete the definition of each word.

1. A **helmet** is something you wear to protect your _____.
   a. hands   b. head   c. legs

2. A **ladder** is something you use to go _____.
   a. back   b. fast   c. up

3. A **rope** is a very strong, thick _____.
   a. rock   b. string   c. cloth

4. A **friendly** person is _____ and acts like a friend.
   a. smart   b. kind   c. handsome

5. A **sight** is something you can _____.
   a. hear   b. see   c. taste

6. Nature is everything that is not made by people, such as _____.
   a. buildings   b. cars   c. plants

B. Choose the best answer to complete each sentence.

1. Some birds are flying (above / on) our heads.

2. For your (activity / safety), don't swim in the river.

3. He is a new member of the (boss / staff).

4. If you are ready to go out, (put on / take off) your shoes.

5. He sat down (between / through) me and my sister.

6. Let's have a(n) (adventure / floor) today.

Sentence Practice

A. **Unscramble the sentences.**

1. (There are / between / ropes / the trees).

⇨ _____

2. (at high speeds / You / along the ropes / slide).

⇨ _____

3. (You / the sights and sounds / of the jungle / can enjoy).

⇨ _____

4. (you / Friendly / take / staff members / into the rainforest).

⇨ _____

B. **Match the sentence parts.**

1. Do you want to fly   •   • high in the trees.

2. There are wooden floors   •   • above the ground!

3. At times, you are 100 meters •   • it's safe.

4. But don't worry –   •   • through the treetops?

C. **Translate each sentence into your language.**

1. Flight of the Gibbon is an adventure activity for nature lovers.

⇨ _____

2. With ropes and ladders, you can go from tree to tree just like a gibbon.

⇨ _____

3. Before you start the adventure, you put on safety clothing and a helmet.

⇨ _____

Vocabulary Practice

A. Choose the best answer to complete the definition of each word.

1. If you **push** something, you use your hands or body to _____ it.

   a. fly   b. move   c. run

2. If you do something **quickly**, you do it _____.

   a. fast   b. quietly   c. many times

3. If something **falls**, it moves _____.

   a. around   b. down   c. up

4. If you **explain** something, you make it _____ to understand.

   a. easy   b. fun   c. important

5. If something is **flat**, it doesn't have _____.

   a. colors   b. bumps   c. sounds

6. A **large** thing is something that is _____ in size.

   a. big   b. medium   c. small

B. Choose the best answer to complete each sentence.

1. The man jumped out of the plane while wearing a (balloon / parachute).

2. The boats are passing (under / over) the bridge.

3. A strange thing (had / happened) that night.

4. The scientist is doing an (experiment / adventure) with plants.

5. I go to the (different / same) school as my cousin.

6. We learned about insects in (science / music) class.

Sentence Practice

A. Unscramble the sentences.

1. (it / does / Why / happen)?

⇨ _____

2. (She / a ball of paper / gives / to Robert).

⇨ _____

3. (Mindy and Robert / their pieces of paper / drop / At the same time,).

⇨ _____

4. (Because / under it, / it falls / pushes up / more slowly / more air).

⇨ _____

B. Match the sentence parts.

1. Let's do • • quickly to the ground.

2. Robert's paper ball falls • • an experiment.

3. Mindy's flat piece of paper • • a parachute!

4. It's just like • • falls down slowly.

C. Translate each sentence into your language.

1. She asks Mindy and Robert to help her.

⇨ _____

2. She gives a flat piece of paper to Mindy.

⇨ _____

3. Mindy's paper is large and flat, so more air is under it.

⇨ _____

Vocabulary Practice

A. Choose the best answer to complete the definition of each word.

1. If you **mix** two things, you make them become _____ .

   a. one   b. bad   c. colorful

2. Vinegar is a liquid that tastes _____ .

   a. sour   b. spicy   c. sweet

3. If something is **warm**, it is a little _____ .

   a. wet   b. cold   c. hot

4. Flour is white powder that you can use for making _____ .

   a. bread   b. chocolate   c. tea

5. If you **pour** something, you make it _____ from one place to another.

   a. bake   b. flow   c. stand

6. Detergent is something that you use for _____ clothes or dishes.

   a. buying   b. making   c. washing

B. Choose the best answer to complete each sentence.

1. Please bring me a (bottle / piece) of water.

2. Put the cookie (dough / powder) in the oven.

3. These (natural / plastic) flowers look real.

4. (Lava / Rock) is flowing quickly down the mountain.

5. Smoke is coming out of the (plant / volcano).

6. I like the (shape / sight) of the table, but I don't like its color.

Sentence Practice

A. Unscramble the sentences.

1. (volcano / Make / own / your)!

⇨ _____

2. (at home / to try / a fun science experiment / Do you want)?

⇨ _____

3. (into the bottle / Get / some vinegar / it / and slowly pour).

⇨ _____

4. (your hands / the dough / Use / to make).

⇨ _____

B. Match the sentence parts.

1. Make • • in a pan.

2. Pour warm water • • some dough.

3. Add red food coloring • • into the bottle.

4. Stand a plastic soda bottle • • to make the lava red.

C. Translate each sentence into your language.

1. Watch out! Here comes the lava!

⇨ _____

2. Put the dough around the bottle in a volcano shape.

⇨ _____

3. Add a few drops of detergent and two tablespoons of baking soda.

⇨ _____

Vocabulary Practice

A. Choose the best answer to complete the definition of each word.

1. Fur is the thick, soft _____ of an animal.

    a. body   b. bone   c. hair

2. A **stripe** is a long _____ of color.

    a. circle   b. line   c. wall

3. If you **kick** something, you hit it with your _____.

    a. arm   b. foot   c. head

4. To **arrive** is to _____ a place.

    a. come to   b. leave for   c. live in

5. If you **build** something, you _____ it.

    a. make   b. want   c. use

6. If you are **without** something, you don't _____ it.

    a. have   b. like   c. forget

B. Choose the best answer to complete each sentence.

1. The dog (guards / stands) our house.

2. Catch the ball with (both / left) hands.

3. I saw two boys (fighting / starting) on the playground.

4. I fell on my (eyes / bottom) on the ice.

5. She is (friendly / selfish), so she doesn't have any friends.

6. I was (angry / excited) because my sister lost my MP3 player.

Sentence Practice

A. Unscramble the sentences.

1. (was / there / a selfish baboon / Long ago,).

⇨ _____

2. (is / everyone / This water / for).

⇨ _____

3. (at night / a fire / the waterhole / even built / and guarded / He).

⇨ _____

4. (the zebra / white fur / Back then, / had / without stripes).

⇨ _____

B. Match the sentence parts.

1. As he came near,　　•　　　　　•　arrived.

2. One day, a zebra　　•　　　　　•　the baboon hard.

3. The zebra kicked　　•　　　　　•　the baboon jumped up.

4. They both fell　　•　　　　　•　into the baboon's fire.

C. Translate each sentence into your language.

1. The baboon guarded a waterhole, so other animals couldn't drink there.

⇨ _____

2. The zebra burned his fur and the baboon burned his bottom.

⇨ _____

3. That's why the zebra has black stripes and the baboon has a red bottom.

⇨ _____

Vocabulary Practice

A. Choose the best answer to complete the definition of each word.

1. A **lamb** is a _____ sheep.

a. short   b. wild   c. young

2. Beef is the meat from a _____.

a. cow   b. duck   c. pig

3. A **cub** is the _____ of a wild animal.

a. baby   b. friend   c. mom

4. If you **attack** someone, you try to _____ the person.

a. help   b. hate   c. hurt

5. A **farm** is a place used for keeping _____ and growing food.

a. animals   b. flowers   c. books

6. A **zoo** is a place where you can _____ many kinds of animals.

a. take   b. see   c. buy

B. Choose the best answer to complete each sentence.

1. My sister and I look very (different / both).

2. I go to the movies once a (time / month).

3. I like (carrots / meat), but I don't like vegetables.

4. There is a drop of (blood / bottle) on his shirt.

5. He ate the (same / whole) cake, so I couldn't eat anything.

6. When he's really sick, he (throws up / throws away).

Sentence Practice

A. Unscramble the sentences.

1. (love / lions / lots of meat / Usually, / to eat).

⇨ _____

2. (Her best friend / called Becky / a lamb / was).

⇨ _____

3. (with / She / other animals / friends / even made).

⇨ _____

4. (didn't even drink / milk / She / mixed with beef blood).

⇨ _____

B. Match the sentence parts.

1. Little Tyke •   • a lion cub.

2. Little Tyke was •   • to have meat.

3. She didn't want •   • threw up.

4. The two animals played •   • together their whole lives.

C. Translate each sentence into your language.

1. Sadly, Little Tyke's mother attacked her when she was born.

⇨ _____

2. A married couple took Little Tyke to their farm.

⇨ _____

3. When Little Tyke was three months old, the couple gave her some meat.

⇨ _____

Vocabulary Practice

A. Choose the best answer to complete the definition of each word.

1. If something is **burning**, it is on _____.

a. fire   b. gas   c. water

2. A **hero** is a person who does great things for _____.

a. money   b. a name   c. people

3. If something is **dangerous**, it can _____ you.

a. hurt   b. push   c. save

4. A **firefighter** is someone who _____ fires.

a. has   b. puts   c. stops

5. To **spend** is to _____ your time or money.

a. buy   b. have   c. use

6. A **forest** is a place that is covered with _____ and bushes.

a. birds   b. rocks   c. trees

B. Choose the best answer to complete each sentence.

1. (Imagine / Watch) that you are flying.

2. The movie was (exciting / scary), but I liked it.

3. Many people helped to (put out / put on) the fire.

4. He was really worried, but he tried to look (afraid / calm).

5. You have to wear safety (ball / equipment) for this sport.

6. She was very (brave / kind) to fight the shark.

Sentence Practice

A. Unscramble the sentences.

1. (a usual day's work / smokejumpers / It's / for)!

⇨ _____

2. (I / about smokejumpers / a TV show / watched / Today).

⇨ _____

3. (looked / the big forest fires / On the TV show, / really scary).

⇨ _____

4. (50 kg of equipment / with them / Smokejumpers / carry around).

⇨ _____

B. Match the sentence parts.

1. Smokejumpers are •   • they are heroes!

2. They put out •   • special firefighters.

3. They stay calm •   • dangerous forest fires.

4. I think •   • when they are working.

C. Translate each sentence into your language.

1. Can you imagine jumping from a plane into a burning forest?

⇨ _____

2. To get to the fires, they wear parachutes and jump from planes.

⇨ _____

3. Sometimes, smokejumpers spend up to five days fighting forest fires.

⇨ _____

Vocabulary Practice

A. Choose the best answer to complete the definition of each word.

1. An **actress** is a woman who _____ in a movie or play.

a. acts   b. makes   c. sings

2. A **young** person has not lived very _____ .

a. little   b. long   c. strong

3. If someone is **famous**, very many people _____ who the person is.

a. know   b. meet   c. hate

4. An **award** is a prize that you _____ when you do something very well.

a. get   b. give   c. make

5. A **college** is a school that you go to after _____ school.

a. elementary   b. middle   c. high

6. An **exam** is a _____ to see how much you know about a subject.

a. note   b. test   c. play

B. Choose the best answer to complete each sentence.

1. I (first / one) saw him at the party.

2. He (had / won) a gold medal at the Olympics.

3. I have (one / several) pencils, so you can have one of them.

4. My sister is very (smart / stupid) and always gets good grades.

5. My favorite singer (appeared / saw) on TV yesterday.

6. She didn't want to eat out, so she cooked dinner (instead / finally).

Sentence Practice

A. Unscramble the sentences.

1. (studied / Instead / for her exams / she)!

⇨ _____

2. (being a movie star / Being smart / better than / is).

⇨ _____

3. (she was young / Natalie Portman / acting / started / when).

⇨ _____

4. (more important / acting / College / is / than).

⇨ _____

B. Match the sentence parts.

1. She played   •   • a queen in the movies.

2. She won   •   • to Harvard University.

3. She still   •   • studied hard at school.

4. Portman went   •   • several awards as an actress.

C. Translate each sentence into your language.

1. After she was in the *Star Wars* movies, she became famous.

⇨ _____

2. She was only 13 when she appeared in her first movie, *Leon*.

⇨ _____

3. She didn't even go to see the first showing of her *Star Wars* movie.

⇨ _____

Vocabulary Practice

A. Choose the best answer to complete the definition of each word.

1. If something is **wet**, it is covered in _____ .
   a. paper   b. dirt   c. water

2. A **principal** is the head teacher of a _____ .
   a. building   b. company   c. school

3. A **footprint** is a mark made by a foot or _____ .
   a. leg   b. finger   c. shoe

4. A **mall** is a large building that has many _____ inside.
   a. cinemas   b. offices   c. stores

5. If you **meet** someone, you go to a place and _____ the person.
   a. hear   b. see   c. call

6. If something is **narrow**, it is _____ from one side to the other.
   a. high   b. far   c. small

B. Choose the best answer to complete each sentence.

1. He (seemed / showed) me a picture of his family.

2. No one was in the room yet because I came too (early / quietly).

3. This floor is made of (cement / water).

4. I heard (somebody / something) calling my name.

5. This river is very (clear / wide), so you can't swim across it.

6. A woman is selling snacks on the (crosswalk / sidewalk).

Sentence Practice

A. Unscramble the sentences.

1. (fast / She / walk / couldn't).

⇨ _____

2. (I / it / who did / knew / Then).

⇨ _____

3. (together / Let's / have / some ice cream).

⇨ _____

4. (in / Somebody / jumped / this wet cement)!

⇨ _____

B. Match the sentence parts.

1. I saw   •   • to go home.

2. I wanted   •   • at the sidewalk.

3. He was looking •   • a broken leg.

4. Poor Sara had •   • two narrow footprints there.

C. Translate each sentence into your language.

1. Rachel showed me her new shoes.

⇨ _____

2. On my way home, I saw the school principal outside the school.

⇨ _____

3. I only saw Rachel, Sara, and Tina here earlier.

⇨ _____

Vocabulary Practice

A. Choose the best answer to complete the definition of each word.

1. To **create** is to make something _____.

a. big   b. fun   c. new

2. Someone who is **thin** is not _____.

a. healthy   b. fat   c. tall

3. If you **visit** a place, you go and spend _____ there.

a. energy   b. money   c. time

4. If you **solve** a problem, you find the correct _____ to it.

a. answer   b. exam   c. question

5. A **museum** is a building where you can _____ many interesting things.

a. buy   b. make   c. see

6. If something is **real**, it is not just _____.

a. sold   b. moved   c. imagined

B. Choose the best answer to complete each sentence.

1. J. K. Rowling is a (British / England) writer.

2. She came to see her son's school (book / play).

3. The magician wears a cool (hat / head).

4. Please do not (smoke / swim) inside the building.

5. The (detective / doctor) is trying to catch the bad guy.

6. Seventy (part / percent) of my books are mystery novels.

Sentence Practice

A. Unscramble the sentences.

1. (a hunting hat / a pipe / He / and smokes / often wears).

⇨ _____

2. (Although / a real person / very famous, / he is / he is not).

⇨ _____

3. (in 1887 / created / Sherlock Holmes / Arthur Conan Doyle).

⇨ _____

4. (him / around the world / love / People).

⇨ _____

B. Match the sentence parts.

1. Sherlock Holmes ·   · is a British detective.

2. He lives ·   · tall and thin.

3. Holmes is ·   · with his friend Watson.

4. Watson helps Holmes ·   · solve mysteries.

C. Translate each sentence into your language.

1. There are many books, TV shows, plays, and movies about him.

⇨ _____

2. In a newspaper story, 21 percent of British people thought he was real!

⇨ _____

3. Today, fans of Sherlock Holmes can visit the Sherlock Holmes Museum.

⇨ _____

Memo

Memo

Memo

Reading Clue is a three-level reading series for high beginners. This series helps students to read passages smoothly and quickly while understanding the main ideas presented in them. ***Reading Clue*** contains a balance of fiction and nonfiction texts combined with systematic activities. All readings are based on word lists that have been carefully selected to expand students' vocabulary and develop their reading fluency. Throughout ***Reading Clue***, students will master the basic skills needed in reading comprehension. Engaging illustrations and reading passages with meaningful follow-up activities are designed to attract the interest of students and make learning enjoyable.

Features:

- **Compelling, theme-based topics:** to stimulate students' intellectual curiosity
- **Meaningful vocabulary activities:** to help students learn key words through engaging sentences and illustrations
- **Emphasis on summarizing activities:** to help students structure their thinking with graphic organizers and follow-up summarizing activities
- **Attractive images:** to maximize students' imagination
- **Workbook for vocabulary and sentence practice:** to expand students' vocabulary and allow them to review the reading passages

Components:

- ***Reading Clue*** Student Book (Workbook and Audio CD are included)

Online Resources: www.nebuildandgrow.co.kr (for students)
www.netutor.co.kr (for teachers)

- MP3 files / Vocabulary lists / Answer keys and translation

Reading Clue Series:

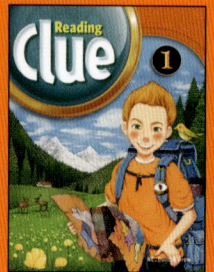 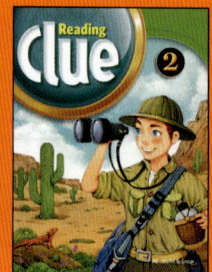 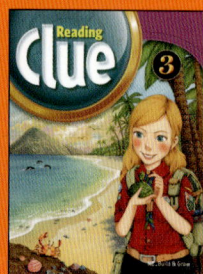

<100-110 words>   <110-120 words>   <120-130 words>